CHRISTOPHER TUGENDHAT

The Worm in the Apple

A History of the Conservative Party and
Europe from Churchill to Cameron

Published in 2022 by
Haus Publishing Ltd
4 Cinnamon Row
London SW11 3TW

Copyright © Christopher Tugendhat, 2022

A CIP catalogue for this book is available from the British Library

The moral right of the author has been asserted

ISBN 978-1-913368-53-1
eISBN 978-1-913368-54-8

Typeset in Sabon by MacGuru Ltd

Printed in the UK by Clays Ltd, Elcograf S.p.A.

www.hauspublishing.com
@HausPublishing

For Julia, for ever and always

Contents

Introduction

The controversy within the Conservative Party over Europe was for sixty-five years an enduring drama of British politics – from Churchill's decision not to join the original European Coal and Steel Community (ECSC) in 1951 to Cameron's decision to hold an In/Out referendum in 2016. Other incidents came and went. It was always there, sometimes in the foreground, at others behind the scenes. It destabilised British foreign policy, corroded the body politic, and destroyed several of the party's leaders.

The drama was sustained by a sequence of ifs. If Churchill, and Eden, had not turned their backs on the original enterprise in the 1950s; if Macmillan in 1961 and Heath in 1973 had not rejected advice to come clean with the people about the sovereignty implications of membership; if President Valéry Giscard d'Estaing of France and Chancellor Helmut Schmidt of West Germany had not tried to browbeat Margaret Thatcher when she became prime minister in 1979; if her fall in 1990 had not left a legacy of bitterness about Europe; if she had not undermined her successor, John Major, after he had negotiated the Maastricht Treaty in 1992; if, after 1997, the Conservative Party had not paved the way for UKIP and fallen in thrall to its agenda; if immigration into Britain from other European Union (EU) countries had not increased so much after the enlargement of the EU in 2004; if, if, if...

These possibilities and how they panned out created a deep, grumbling discontent – the worm in the apple – that, over time, turned the Conservative Party and, by extension, a significant section of the electorate against British membership of the EU. While the outward form of the membership remained unchanged, the worm ate away at its legitimacy. To understand why Britain voted to leave in 2016, it is necessary to understand the arguments and divisions within the Conservative Party that began under Churchill and reached their apotheosis under Cameron. They are by no means the whole story, but they are an important part of it.

In 1972, as a Conservative MP, I voted in favour of the highly contentious European Communities Act, which enabled Britain to join the European Economic Community (EEC) on 1 January 1973. In the 1975 referendum, I campaigned with other members of my party for Britain to remain a member. When Thatcher was prime minister, I was a European commissioner in Brussels. When I returned to Britain in 1985, I wrote a book about the future of Europe.[1] Since the early 1990s, I have been a member of the House of Lords, participating in debates on European issues. In the 2016 referendum, I voted to remain.

Now, fifty years after the epic Parliamentary battles generated by the 1972 act, I explain how the worm entered the apple; why it flourished; how the apple might have been saved; and the factors, going back over many decades, that contributed to the result of the 2016 referendum and so to British withdrawal.

1

Missed Opportunities 1946–1959

Dean Acheson, who served as American secretary of state during the post-war years, entitled his autobiography *Present at the Creation*. He was justified in doing so. During the decade after 1945, almost all the great international organisations with which we are familiar today, or their predecessors, were established – the United Nations, the International Monetary Fund, the World Bank, the World Trade Organization, the World Health Organization, the North Atlantic Treaty Organization, the European Union, and others. In all bar one of these that have had Britain as a member, British ministers and officials played a major role in setting them up and forming their working practices.

The exception is the European Union (EU), which began with the European Coal and Steel Community (ECSC), established in 1951 by France, West Germany,[1] Italy, the Netherlands, Belgium, and Luxembourg. The same six countries then created the European Economic Community (EEC) in 1957; after various enlargements and reforms, this became the EU in 1993.[2] In the aftermath of the war, the architects of those institutions would have welcomed British participation. But both Clement Attlee's Labour government and its Conservative successor under Winston Churchill declined to join the ECSC, and Anthony Eden's Conservative administration decided against the EEC. When, in 1961, Harold Macmillan wanted to reverse that decision, General de Gaulle, as president of France, imposed a veto.

A second attempt in 1967 by the Labour prime minister Harold Wilson met the same fate. Only after the general's departure was the Conservative Ted Heath able to lead Britain into the EEC on 1 January 1973.

From this simple fact stems many of the grievances and misunderstandings that bedevilled Britain's relationship with the other member states and the European Commission during the next forty-seven years. By the time Britain joined, the essential character of the organisation, its institutional structure, its working methods, its core policies, and its aspirations had been established. So, too, had the language and imagery in which those aspirations were clothed. There had been no British input. It had been formed by alien ideas and principles and was based on unfamiliar practices – mainly, but not only, French.

In other international organisations, British ministers and officials felt instantly at home; in the EEC, everything was unfamiliar. Over time – by which I mean decades – as officials built their careers dealing with Brussels and negotiating with the other member states, sections of the British civil service became as familiar with the system as those of other countries. This was never true of ministers. It is striking, however, how often they changed their minds, usually grudgingly and without enthusiasm, as they discovered how British interests, both within Europe and beyond, could be furthered and maintained through the endless negotiations that characterise the EU's working methods.

As for the British public, the consequences of our late arrival quickly became apparent to me when, in 1977, as a newly appointed commissioner, I began addressing audiences in both Britain and other member states on European issues. I found that most people in this country simply did not feel the same sense of commitment towards, or faith in, the European venture as their counterparts in other European countries.

The differences were fundamental. People in other member states, not everyone everywhere but a solid and sufficient core, regarded the European venture as a means of overcoming the historic rivalries of the past that had led to war, and adapting them to peaceful purposes for which it was worth sacrificing elements of national sovereignty. A belief that I shared. The British, apart from a small minority, were untouched by this sense of historic purpose and regarded joining the Common Market, as they generally then called the EEC, in purely economic and utilitarian terms.

Whereas others saw the somewhat vague aspiration of 'ever closer union' as an expression of their desire to banish the past and create a better future, many in Britain regarded it as a threat to their sense of identity and national sovereignty. This was at least as true of Conservatives as of anyone else, even though it had been Heath's Conservative government that had taken Britain into the EEC, and the Conservative Party, by then led by Margaret Thatcher, that had contributed more than any other to winning the 1975 referendum that confirmed British membership. I recognised, in the light of these differences, that building a firm base of support for the EEC in Britain, let alone generating enthusiasm, would be an uphill struggle. I did not expect to live to see it end in failure. And I certainly did not expect it to be another Conservative prime minister who would lead the country out with the overwhelming support of his party, the party of which I have been a member since the 1950s.

Could it have been otherwise? Could Britain have been a founder member? Could Britain even have provided the foundation on which the whole edifice of post-war Europe was built?

In 1945 Britain's reputation in Europe stood at an all-time high. It was the only European country to have fought against Nazi Germany from the beginning to the end of the war and never to have been defeated or occupied. It had stood alone in

1940 and 1941 and later, in conjunction with the United States and the Soviet Union, had played a major role in liberating the continent in 1944 and 1945. Jean Monnet, the Frenchman whose vision and behind-the-scenes political skills played a crucial role in the formation of the ECSC, had initially turned to Britain as 'a nucleus around which a European Community might be formed'. He saw it as 'the one great power in Europe which was then in a position to take on such responsibility'.[3] Having served as a senior French official in London during the First World War and again in London and Washington during the Second, he was well connected across the British establishment, but when he informally floated his ideas in London they fell on deaf ears.

General de Gaulle, too, initially regarded Britain as indispensable. After Churchill had made a great speech in Zurich in September 1946 calling for a united Europe based on the twin pillars of France and Germany,[4] he sought the views of the general, who, like him, was at that time out of office. De Gaulle replied that 'if French support was to be won for the idea of European union, France must come in as a founder partner with Britain. Moreover, the two countries must reach a precise understanding with one another upon the attitude to be adopted towards Germany before any approaches were made to the latter'.[5]

Why, then, did it not happen? Why did Britain, under a Labour government from 1945 to 1951 and thereafter a Conservative one, not become an influential founder member of what is now the EU?

The answer is to be found in the nature of British politics and the country's international relations agenda during the years after the Second World War. The overwhelming international preoccupation of British ministers and politicians of both parties was the Cold War with its front line in Germany. There, the armies of the Western Alliance, led by the United States and including a large British contingent, faced those of the Soviet bloc, each side armed with nuclear weapons ready for instant use. In 1948 and 1949 the threat of war seemed very close. In February 1948 the Soviet Union, already in control of most of Eastern Europe, took over Czechoslovakia. Then, from June 1948 until May 1949, the Soviet army blockaded Berlin and the American, British, and French forces occupying the city. As the Allied air forces flew in supplies of food and other necessities on a daily basis, the world lived on tenterhooks.

The threat of war continued into the 1950s and beyond. In his history of the period, *Having it So Good*, Peter Hennessy gives an example of the type of question the Cold War obliged the Cabinet to consider. In 1954, the top-secret Strath Committee 'estimated that ten ten-megaton Soviet H-bombs dropped on the UK would kill 12 million people and seriously injure a further 4 million (nearly a third of the population) even before the poisonous effects of radioactive fallout spread across the country'.[6]

On defence matters Britain took the lead in post-war Europe. It played a key role in the formation and development of the North Atlantic Treaty Organization (NATO). It was similarly constructive in the creation and running of the structures for administering the Marshall Plan by means of which the United States contributed massive financial aid for the reconstruction of the Western European economies, including Britain's. To the Americans and British alike, NATO and the Marshall Plan were complementary means of helping Western Europe to withstand the Soviet threat. But the British were fundamentally not interested in, and did not take seriously, the efforts of political leaders on the continent to establish economic structures designed to underpin a drive towards political unity. As will become apparent, the Americans took a different view.

In Westminster and Whitehall, those efforts had to jostle for attention with a host of other issues that in the eyes of British ministers commanded more immediate attention. Prominent among them between 1951 (when the Conservatives returned to power after six years of Labour government) and 1954 was the Korean War, in which 15,000 British troops fought alongside the Americans against the North Koreans and Chinese. Another that aroused very strong feelings within the Conservative Party was the saga of the Suez Canal. This began with a heated debate over whether Britain should give up its treaty rights and influence in Egypt and withdraw from its military base guarding the Suez Canal, as Churchill, to the fury of some of his backbenchers, decided to do in 1954. It reached its zenith when the Egyptians nationalised the canal in July 1956, thereby triggering a joint British and French military operation to re-take it in November of that year. The humiliating failure of this operation, as a result of intense American economic pressure on the British, led, as usually happens after a military defeat, to bitter recriminations. Other problems included Iran's nationalisation in 1951 of the British oil refinery at Abadan, then regarded as a vital national interest, and the colonial uprisings in Kenya, Cyprus, and Malaya.

Besides this press of events, there was a widespread view across the political spectrum that the war had shown Britain to be qualitatively different from other European countries and that their rivalries were such that it was most unlikely that they would ever be able to put together any lasting arrangements among themselves. Far more important than closer ties with Europe, according to this view, were relations with the Commonwealth and the United States, who had proved their reliability during the war. This was also the opinion of most of the senior officials in the Foreign Office and the Treasury. Events were to show that it was a great mistake to underestimate the Europeans in this way, but it is understandable that those who had lived through the war should have thought as they did.

While leading the party in opposition from 1945 to 1951, Churchill made important and attention-grabbing speeches about the future of Europe, but, as the 1951 Conservative election manifesto spelt out, this subject was neither his nor his party's principal non-domestic concern. Top of the list came 'the safety, progress and cohesion of the British Empire and Commonwealth',[7] next the United States, and, in third place, Europe. As Roy Jenkins explains in his biography of Churchill, leading continental figures in the drive towards a united Europe, such as Monnet, the Belgian Paul-Henri Spaak, and the German chancellor, Konrad Adenauer, were just as committed to a close relationship with the United States as he; given Europe's dependence on the United States for its defence, they had to be. But whereas their priority was the drive towards European union, Churchill's was the Commonwealth.[8]

Therein lay obvious scope for misunderstanding once work began on translating words into action. It was enhanced by the fact that men like Monnet thought in terms of structures with federalist potential while neither Churchill nor other Conservatives interested in Europe's future ever sought to define what they had in mind. Macmillan, who was among the most active in what has been described as the Europeanist group, explained this in terms of continentals preferring to proceed on an *a priori* basis and the British preferring an *a posteriori* approach. But the difference was deeper than that. Churchill was clear in his rejection of anything that smacked of federalism, and there was no support for it among even the most Europeanist Conservatives.

In 1949, in a speech at a rally of the United Europe Movement, which he had himself founded two years earlier, Churchill set out his thinking in these words:

Britain is an integral part of Europe and we mean to play our part in the revival of her prosperity and greatness. But

Britain cannot be thought of as a single state in isolation. She is the founder and centre of a worldwide Empire and Commonwealth. We shall never do anything to weaken the ties of blood, sentiment and tradition and common interests that unite us with members of the British family of nations.[9]

The movement was an all-party operation with Labour and Liberal members, but the balance was very much on the Conservative side, with several future Cabinet ministers, including Macmillan, Duncan Sandys (Churchill's son-in-law), Peter Thorneycroft, and David Eccles, among its most active members. Other prominent Conservatives took care to signal their reservations, notably Eden, the former foreign secretary and Churchill's heir apparent, and Rab Butler, who was in charge of the party's policymaking. Many other Conservative MPs shared their misgivings, fearing that getting too close to Europe would weaken links with the Commonwealth.

On the continent, audiences did not pick up on the priority that Churchill attached to the Commonwealth connection when he spoke about Europe. It was his clarion calls for European reconciliation and unity that they heard. At Zurich in September 1946, in the speech mentioned above, just sixteen months after VE Day, he had created a sensation with his call for 'a kind of United States of Europe'. This would, he explained, be based on a partnership between France and Germany: 'The first step in the re-creation of the European family must be a partnership between France and Germany. In this way only can France recover the moral and cultural leadership of Europe. There can be no revival of Europe without a spiritually great France and spiritually great Germany.'[10] Nothing did more to launch the concept of a united Europe as an objective to be worked towards, as distinct from the stuff of dreams, than this speech. The fact that it contained a paragraph stating that Britain and the Commonwealth would be facilitators and partners, along with the United States, rather than participants, was easily overlooked.

In the second of his two great 1940s European speeches at The Hague in 1948, Churchill rejoiced in the progress made towards the Zurich objective. In particular, he welcomed the recently agreed Charter of Human Rights, which owed much to the work of his Conservative colleague Sir David Maxwell Fyfe (later, as Lord Kilmuir, to become Lord Chancellor in Macmillan's government), who went on to help bring the European Convention on Human Rights into being. He also blurred the distinction between Britain and the countries that would be involved in creating a united Europe. In a section describing his vision of a world government based on a number of groups, he saw 'the vast Soviet Union forming one of these groups. The Council of Europe, including Great Britain with her Empire and Commonwealth would be another,' and 'the United States and her sister republics in the Western Hemisphere' would be a third.[11]

As a project designed to achieve European unity based on a partnership between France and Germany, the proposal to create the ECSC, launched by the French government in 1950, could be described as giving practical effect to Churchill's call. As an explicitly supranational, or federalist, project, it was, however, fundamentally different from anything he would have put forward. It was the brainchild of Monnet, at that time in charge of the French Commissariat général du Plan, the central planning agency widely credited with playing a key role in France's rapid post-war economic recovery.

From this vantage point Monnet foresaw that, although Germany was still under occupation by Britain, France, the United States, and the Soviet Union, its economy would in the long run again outstrip that of France and become the most powerful in Europe. He feared that this would reawaken France's historical fears and could become another casus belli. To forestall that danger, he conceived an original and ambitious plan. The two countries would pool their coal and steel resources, in those days the sinews of war and the commanding heights of the economy. These would then be placed under the sovereign control of a high authority in an organisation that other countries would be free to join.

The genesis of Monnet's scheme can be found in ideas circulating on the continent between the wars, but as a practical proposition for governments to consider, it was revolutionary. Its beauty lay in its symmetry. In the long term, it sought to protect France against the consequences of a resurgent Germany. In the short term, it provided Germany – or at least the Federal Republic of Germany that had been formed from the amalgamation of the British, French, and American zones – with the opportunity to work with France and the other participating countries in an area of vital economic importance.

The West German government agreed with alacrity. To be treated as an equal so soon after the war fulfilled its dearest diplomatic wish. It also helped to confer legitimacy on the new state in the eyes of its citizens and to counter persistent Soviet attempts to undermine it.

Monnet's scheme was equally appealing to the deepest instincts of the French foreign minister Robert Schuman, a native of Alsace-Lorraine. Three times in the previous eighty years that territory had been fought over by France and Germany and changed hands between them. With this background, he immediately grasped the strategic and historic significance of what Monnet was proposing and adopted the scheme as his own. By the early months of 1950, it had become French government policy as the Schuman Plan.

The next step was to present the plan to the other two Western occupying powers, which was set to be done at a tripartite conference already scheduled to be held in London on 9 May 1950. As the US secretary of state, Acheson, was due to pass through Paris on his way to London, Monnet, who knew him from his time in Washington during the war, and Schuman decided to take him into their confidence before the plan was officially announced. When the British foreign secretary, Ernest Bevin, realised that Acheson had this prior knowledge, he was understandably outraged, and the talks got off to a difficult start. Thereafter, the plan was subjected to detailed scrutiny by British ministers and officials and debated in Parliament.

The immediate question was not whether Britain should sign up to the plan but whether it should join France, and other countries that declared their interest, in talks aimed at creating the organisational structure and rules required to bring it into being. There were genuine doubts in London about whether such a novel idea could be made to work. There were qualms too about whether it would be in the interests of the British coal and steel industries, which at the time accounted for half the coal and a third of the steel produced in Europe, to participate. Those questions aside, the Labour government regarded its nationalisation of the coal industry in 1946 as one of its greatest achievements and looked forward to nationalising steel as well. The idea of subjecting them to some sort of pan-European supervision was deeply unattractive. Besides which, both Labour and Conservative MPs foresaw great difficulties in the event of job losses arising as a result of decisions taken by a body outside this country.

Whether or not these problems could have been resolved, the deal-breaker was the federal nature of the plan. A note sent by the British government to Paris during the scrutiny process makes this clear. Its key words read:

It should be realised ... that if the French Government intend to insist on a commitment to pool resources and set up an authority with certain sovereign powers as a condition to joining the talks, His Majesty's Government would reluctantly be unable to accept such a condition. His Majesty's Government would greatly regret such an outcome.[12]

Thus, a precedent was set that would constantly recur in Britain's relations with the other member states throughout the years of its membership of the EU. Whenever a significant proposal was tabled by the Commission or another member state, the British would agonise over its implications for sovereignty. As the years went by, the sovereignty issue would come to loom ever larger in the domestic debate about the merits and demerits of membership and to resonate particularly strongly among Conservatives.

Acheson was convinced from the outset that it was in the interests of both Britain and the United States for Britain to take part in the talks, and he tried to persuade the Attlee government to do so. President Truman intervened personally with a public statement welcoming the plan as 'an act of constructive statesmanship' and a 'demonstration of French leadership in the solution of the problems of Europe'.[13] Some twenty years later, Acheson wrote in his autobiography that 'Britain made her great mistake of the post-war period by refusing to join in negotiating the Schuman Plan.'[14]

I agree with that judgement. The ECSC and later the EEC provided the framework within which France and Germany buried the hatchet and learned over time how to work closely together. It is hard to recall now how difficult that was at the beginning and how much work it required on the part of the leaders of the two countries. If Britain had been present at this creation, might it not have been able to act as a catalyst? Could Britain in this way have become an indispensable member of the team? Given the immense prestige and moral authority it enjoyed as a result of the war, enhanced by Churchill's Zurich and Hague speeches, that cannot be dismissed as an impossible dream. Moreover, if Britain had been on the inside when de Gaulle returned to power in France in 1958, the approach of the two countries towards the federalist ambitions of others would have been very similar.

In light of Churchill's Zurich and Hague speeches, many on the continent believed that if he instead of Attlee had been prime minister when the Schuman Plan was launched, Britain would have reacted more positively. They were encouraged in this view by the debate that took place in the House of Commons in June 1950 on whether Britain should participate in the talks. Churchill had criticised the government for its insularity for refusing to do so, and the Conservative Party had voted in favour of participation. Several future Cabinet ministers spoke in favour, including two future prime ministers: Macmillan and, in a well-received maiden speech, Ted Heath, who had been elected to Parliament in the February 1950 general election that had greatly reduced the majority won by Labour in 1945.

Heath's speech was notable for its breadth of vision. Instead of dwelling, like so many others, on the practical difficulties and potential pitfalls of implementing Schuman's plan, he spoke about what it might be able to achieve. He saw it as a means of developing Western Europe's economic potential for the benefit of its citizens, including Britons, and as a bulwark against the Soviet threat. He was excited by the idea of reconciliation between France and Germany. He also grasped the significance of Schuman's visionary idea that economic success would enable Europe 'to pursue the realisation of one of her essential tasks – the development of the African continent',[15] an idea then well ahead of its time. What he did not address was the question of sovereignty.

Other Conservative MPs were unhappy with the leadership's support for accepting the French invitation to engage in talks,

precisely because of the plan's implications for national sovereignty. When the division was called, six defied a three-line whip
and abstained. One was Harry Legge-Bourke, a quintessential
backbone-of-the-party type of backbencher, who later explained
that his position was based on the belief that the Schuman Plan
was 'a move towards European political federation'.[16] Another
was Enoch Powell, now remembered as one of the most out-
spoken opponents of the whole Europe project from the 1970s
on, although he would in fact change his mind about it more
than once before reaching a settled position.

Another general election took place in October 1951 and
returned a Conservative government, with Churchill once again
becoming prime minister, thereby creating an opportunity for
him and his colleagues to do what they had criticised Labour for
not doing. The Treaty of Paris, establishing the ECSC, had been
signed in the previous April by France, West Germany, the Netherlands, Belgium, and Luxembourg – now increasingly known
as 'the Six' – but was not due to come into effect until July 1952.
There was still time for Britain to make a late entry. But time
had moved on. With the Korean War and the rearmament programme uppermost in their minds, the incoming ministers did
not wish to reopen what was bound to be a contentious issue.
Eden, now back at the Foreign Office, supported by Butler at the
Treasury, were against, and their view was backed by most of the
mandarins in Whitehall.

As minister for housing and local government, Macmillan
had portfolio responsibilities far removed from these matters.
He considered resigning in protest at the government's decision
but did not do so. Reflecting on that decision in later life, he concluded that his resignation 'would have been a terrible mistake',
partly because the government had a majority of only sixteen
and partly because there was 'no enthusiasm in the country
whatever for Europe'.[17]

The government's decision came as a great disappointment to all those in the Six who had been inspired by Churchill's speeches and misled as to the true nature of Conservative opinion by those Conservative MPs who attended the Strasbourg meetings of the Consultative Committee of the Council of Europe that had been set up after the Hague meeting. They felt that the British, having provided the initial inspiration for a united Europe, had then let down those trying to put it into practice. Monnet drew the conclusion that Britain 'does not wish to let her domestic life or the development of her resources be influenced by any views other than her own, and certainly not by continental views'.[18] He attributed this to a British belief that in any future conflict, 'continental Europe will be occupied but that she herself, with America, will be able to resist and finally conquer'.[19] Many at that time, both in and outside the Conservative Party, would have agreed with this assessment.

They would have felt vindicated by what happened to the next attempt to carry forward the European project. In the climate of crisis sparked by the Korean War, the United States called for the Western Alliance to be strengthened by the rearmament of West Germany. The French responded with a proposal for the establishment of a European Defence Community, into which German military formations would be incorporated. This provoked such a bitter debate within the Six that for a while it appeared to threaten all the progress made towards reconciliation since the end of the war. Eventually it was rejected by the French themselves. The question of German rearmament was then only resolved when Eden, in the final diplomatic coup of his career, brokered a settlement that linked German rearmament within NATO to a British commitment to station substantial army and air force contingents permanently in West Germany.

In April 1955, after putting off the evil moment for as long as he could, Churchill finally retired. He was succeeded by Eden, who appointed Macmillan foreign secretary and Butler as chancellor of the exchequer. Eden was one of the two most cultivated men to become prime minister during the twentieth century, the other being Arthur Balfour some fifty years earlier. His undergraduate degree at Oxford had been in Persian and Arabic. He loved literature, especially Persian poetry and Shakespeare. He had a deep appreciation of French culture and possessed an art collection that included works by Monet, Degas, Corot, Picasso, and Braque. His diplomatic experience was unrivalled. He was the absolute reverse of a little Englander. He was, however, convinced that the ideas of men like Monnet and Spaak would never work and that it would, in any case, be impossible to mobilise British public opinion in favour of involvement in Europe. In a telling expression of this view, he told his private secretary, Evelyn Shuckburgh, 'What you've got to remember is that if you looked into the post-bag of any English village and examined the letters coming from abroad, ninety per cent would come from way beyond Europe.'[20]

Economics and trading patterns were not Eden's forte. He would have known that the Commonwealth during the early 1950s accounted for 49 per cent of British imports and 54 per cent of British exports, and that its members were therefore collectively Britain's most important trading partners. What he failed to grasp was the economic potential of the Six and how within a very few years they would create a bigger and more dynamic market than the Commonwealth, one that would present both a threat to Britain and an opportunity. He equally failed to grasp the extent to which the Commonwealth countries were chafing against the pre-war Imperial Preference system that governed the terms of intra-Commonwealth trade and wished to loosen their economic links with Britain.

Others were more perceptive. In 1951, on his appointment as president of the Board of Trade, Peter Thorneycroft had asked his permanent secretary whether he believed 'in all this Imperial Preference nonsense'.[21] In the 1954 Reith Lectures, the former ambassador to Washington and chair of Lloyds Bank, Sir Oliver Franks, warned those who advocated a policy of increased Imperial Preference 'that it is out of date and has no chance' of continuing.[22] At the Commonwealth conference in 1956, Macmillan was given a taste of what this meant when confronted by an Australian demand 'to abolish (or whittle away to nothing) UK preferences in Australia, but keep – and improve – their favoured position in our market'.[23]

Whatever Eden's own doubts about a closer alignment with Europe, or those of the British public, economic trends were moving in a direction that demanded a re-think as to where Britain's interests would lie in the future and how they might best be promoted. To stand aside from Europe instead of seeking to influence its evolution, while there was still time, was becoming increasingly dangerous.

Contrary to widespread expectation in London, the collapse of the proposed European Defence Community did not mark the end of the efforts to carry forward the pursuit of European unity through the pooling of economic resources. No sooner had the new ministers in London taken up their portfolios than they were confronted by another far-reaching European initiative. In June 1955 the foreign ministers of the six ECSC countries met at Messina in Sicily, where they discussed how to establish 'a united Europe by the development of common institutions, the gradual fusion of national economies, the creation of a Common Market and the gradual development of ... social policies'.[24] The Belgian foreign minister, Spaak, was put in charge of a committee set up to create the necessary organisational structure to bring this ambitious aspiration into being. He had spent the war years in London as a member of the Belgian government in exile, was strongly pro-British, and immediately invited the British government to send a representative to join his committee.

At a meeting of finance ministers held shortly after the Messina deliberations, Butler provided an indication of the likely British reaction. Famous in British political circles for his subtle and double-edged jokes, he said he understood there had been 'some archaeological excavations going on at an old Sicilian town'.[25] His disdain and the implication that those deliberations had been about digging up the past rather than looking to the future were not well received.

When Butler returned to London, the Cabinet debated how to respond to Spaak's invitation. A majority, led by Eden with Butler's support, did not wish Britain to become involved in any arrangements that might emerge from the discussions among the Six if they in any way resembled those set out in the Messina declaration. Others, notably Macmillan and Thorneycroft, were more open minded. There was a general expectation that in the end the Spaak committee would probably not come up with anything of substance, if only because French industry would not wish to open itself up to German competition in a Common Market. Sir Gladwyn Jebb, the British ambassador in Paris, was a proponent of this view. On the other hand, ministers agreed that it might be dangerous to be left out of the proceedings and that, in case a Common Market should emerge, the opportunity should be taken to influence its form and structure in a manner favourable to Britain.

The high-flying young minister of state at the Foreign Office, Anthony Nutting, an early enthusiast for moves towards European unity, pressed hard to be appointed as the British representative on the Spaak committee, but to no avail.[26] In a gesture that indicated how unimportant the British government regarded the matter to be, Russell Bretherton, a middle-ranking official at the Board of Trade, was sent instead. Many years later,

Thorneycroft, who as president of the Board of Trade had a seat in the Cabinet, told the historian Peter Hennessy how much he regretted not going himself:

> The opinion in the Cabinet was too strongly averse to Europe to commit a Cabinet minister to those negotiations at that time. I wish I had gone. If we had managed to get an accommodation – or to start to get an accommodation with them – the history of Europe would have been very different.[27]

Bretherton soon realised that the Six were in earnest and that the implications for Britain of what they were working towards would be profound. He advised his political masters that a Common Market would be created, and that Britain should try to shape it. His advice was ignored. Instead, he was withdrawn in November 1955, as it was feared that if he remained it would imply a British commitment to the work in progress.

The work of the committee continued until, in April 1956, it produced a report that the Six accepted as the basis for the creation of a Common Market and, in a connected project, a common approach to the peaceful uses of atomic energy. It fell to Macmillan, who had been switched to the Treasury in the previous December, to formulate a British response. He came up with Plan G, as it was always known: a scheme to create a Free Trade Area that would embrace both the Six acting as a single unit and other Western European countries. It would cover all products except foodstuffs, and there would be no common external tariff. Formally unveiled on 3 October 1956, it was presented as a way to avoid a dangerous economic schism from opening up in Western Europe and as a vehicle to create new opportunities for Britain's manufacturing industry.

It immediately ran into trouble on both sides of the Channel. On the continent, it was widely seen as an attempt by the British to stifle at birth the Common Market they had never believed the Six would be able to agree on. Robert Marjolin, who would become the French vice-president when the European Commission was set up in the following year, expressed a widespread view when he later wrote, 'How can one be surprised that in 1956 the British government should have sought in proposing the creation of the European free trade area, to submerge the Common Market in a much larger scheme in which it would have lost its distinctive features?'[28]

In London, as Macmillan recorded in his diary, 'Butler didn't like it',[29] while those backbenchers who were already suspicious of his Europeanist tendencies saw it as being some kind of alternative route to establish closer relations with the Six. The leader of the House of Lords, Lord Salisbury, spoke for the traditionalist wing of the party when he expressed the wish that 'we could return to our old Conservative policy goal of UK producers first, Commonwealth second and foreigners last'.[30]

Before the plan's opponents could mobilise, the Suez Crisis reached its catharsis. The combined British and French military operation to capture the canal involved close collaboration between Eden and the French prime minister, Mollet. There is evidence that Mollet hoped that if, as was confidently expected, they were to share in a military success, the way would be eased for London and Paris to find an agreement on Common Market issues.[31] When the invasion ended in humiliating failure, this hope was dashed. Before Suez there had been a distinct chance that Jebb would be proved right and that France would not, in the end, sign up for what was coming to be called the EEC. After Suez, opinion swung decisively in favour, and on 25 March 1957 the Treaty of Rome establishing the Community was signed.

There is a story that might well be apocryphal, that the West German chancellor, Adenauer, said to Mollet, 'Europe will be your revenge.' Be that as it may, the phrase reflects a significant parting of the ways between British and French views of the world. The conclusion the British drew from the debacle was to stick fast to the United States. The French concluded that they should, if possible, never become too dependent on the United States and must build up a new power base of their own in Europe.

Eden had by then resigned and been replaced in January 1957 by Macmillan, who had triumphed over Butler. In those days there were no leadership elections in the Conservative Party. Whether in government, as in this case, or in opposition, the new leader 'emerged' after a secret and mysterious process of soundings and consultations conducted within the Parliamentary party. What mattered in the final analysis was not just how much support a candidate had, but the intensity of the feeling against him regardless of numbers. During the previous two years, current European issues had been overshadowed by the drama of Suez, and the attitudes of the two candidates towards Europe did not feature in MPs' assessments of their respective merits. Macmillan's role in the Suez drama had been particularly ignominious as he had initially been one of the strongest advocates of the invasion and later, as the American pressure built up, the first to call for a halt. It was, however, a controversy from a different era that torpedoed Butler. In the 1930s, as a junior Foreign Office minister, he had been a prominent appeaser and had remained so even after the outbreak of war. Some of his Parliamentary colleagues would never forgive him for this.

Macmillan's proposal for an overarching free trade area limped on until November 1958. France, by then under the leadership of de Gaulle, refused to countenance it on the grounds that it was incompatible with the development of the EEC. Macmillan then entrusted Reggie Maudling, one of the Conservative Party's rising stars, with the task of negotiating the formation of an alternative grouping to the Six. This he successfully achieved, and in November 1959 a European Free Trade Area comprising Austria, Denmark, Norway, Portugal, Sweden, and Switzerland, along with Britain, was launched.

Commonly known as EFTA, this group's scope was clear. It was confined to industrial free trade and therefore did not give rise to sovereignty concerns. What was not clear was its ultimate purpose – was it to be a bridge to ultimate agreement with the EEC, or was it to be an alternative? The project's future was correspondingly hazy.

Just a month before EFTA was launched, Macmillan had led the Conservatives to a resounding general election victory, thereby staging a remarkable comeback from the low point of Suez and earning the soubriquet of Supermac. With this triumph behind him, he should have been able to secure an enthusiastic response to whatever proposal he brought before the House of Commons. Yet, when the resolution welcoming the EFTA agreement was put to the House, the result was anything but a ringing endorsement. With the Labour Party abstaining, only 183 out of the 365 Conservative MPs voted in favour, with the rest staying away.

In the constituencies, moves towards any kind of shared enterprise with the Six had been causing dissension for some time. Michael Jopling,[32] who would later serve as chief whip and then as minister of agriculture under Margaret Thatcher, recalls how, as a Young Conservative, he earned his first political spurs at the 1957 party conference at Brighton when he helped to thwart an attempt by his local MP, Robin Turton, to persuade the party to oppose the original Free Trade Area proposal.[33]

So ended the first chapter in the fraught story of the Conservative Party's attempts, whether in government or opposition, to come to terms with the question of Europe. The elements that were to cause so much trouble in subsequent decades were already in place – the sensitivity over sovereignty; the sense that

Britain was in a class apart from others, with the corollary that the burden of proof would always be on those in favour of closer links with Europe; the tendency to underestimate the ability of the EEC countries to do what they said they would do; and the potential of the Europe issue to split the party.

2

Macmillan's False Start 1959–1963

The question of whether Britain would try to build on EFTA or seek to join the EEC was answered on 27 July 1961 when, in Macmillan's words, 'the Cabinet agreed that the British Government should make a formal application to accede to the Treaty of Rome'.[1] The decision was announced to Parliament four days later, in a moment that he regarded 'as a turning point in our history'.[2]

This may seem to be a somewhat exaggerated claim for the announcement of an application that ended in failure with de Gaulle's veto, delivered in crushing and humiliating terms on 14 January 1963. But with hindsight we can see that this failure had far-reaching and important effects. On the one hand, the arguments Macmillan deployed in the early 1960s in favour of joining the EEC, and the changes in Britain's economic circumstances to which he drew attention, paved the way in the early 1970s for the government led by Heath to negotiate successfully for British entry. On the other hand, the loss of those ten years meant that Britain was denied the opportunity to influence the crucial early stages of the EEC's development. When it finally joined, the mould was set, and as discussed in Chapter One, the conditions had been created which led to Britain's progressive alienation from the whole European project.

The process leading up to Macmillan's announcement began just over a year earlier. In June 1960, he sent out a questionnaire to all government departments seeking their views on whether Britain should join the EEC, or the Common Market as it was then more generally called. On 27 July, he followed this up with a reshuffle that attracted a great deal of controversy because of the appointment of the Earl of Home, rather than a member of the House of Commons, as foreign secretary. Not since Lord Curzon in the early 1920s had a peer been in charge of the Foreign Office. In the kerfuffle generated by this surprising appointment, it passed unnoticed that Macmillan might be preparing the way for a European initiative. Heath, whose strong views on the subject had been well known since his maiden speech in the ECSC debate in 1950, became a second Cabinet minister in the Foreign Office as Lord Privy Seal in charge of relations with the Common Market. Churchill's two sons-in-law, Duncan Sandys and Christopher Soames, both long-standing Europeanists, were given ministerial responsibility for the two departments thought most likely to cause trouble in the event of a decision being made to apply for membership: Commonwealth Relations for Sandys and Agriculture for Soames.

A major factor in convincing Macmillan that Britain should change its stance had been the collapse in May 1960 of a four-power summit in Paris involving the United States, the Soviet Union, Britain, and France. He had invested a good deal of personal capital in the setting up of this meeting in the hope that it would become the first of a regular series of four-power summits that, over time, would lead to an easing in East–West relations and be seen as his personal contribution to world peace. It collapsed because, just as it was about to begin, the Soviets shot down an American spy plane flying over Russia and refused to continue until they received a suitable apology from President Eisenhower, which he declined to give. Macmillan was devastated. His private secretary, Philip de Zulueta, recorded that 'this was the moment he suddenly realised that Britain counted for nothing: he couldn't move Ike [the nickname by which Eisenhower was universally known] to make a gesture towards Khrushchev [the Soviet leader] and de Gaulle was simply not interested.'[3]

Looking ahead after Paris, Macmillan feared that an increasingly aggressive Soviet Union with the support of China, where the communists under Mao Zedong had taken power in 1949, might secure the upper hand in the Cold War or even precipitate a Third World War. Berlin had always been a dangerous flashpoint, so the building of the Berlin Wall by the Soviet-dominated East German government in the summer of 1961 added credence to this fear, as did Soviet and Chinese activities in the newly independent countries of Africa and Asia. In the light of these developments, Macmillan worried that divisions in Western Europe on matters of trade and economics could spill over into security and diplomatic co-operation, to the detriment of the Western Alliance.

Even within the Western Alliance, Macmillan foresaw potential dangers that could only be avoided by Britain reversing its previous policy. On 9 July 1960 he confided a thought to his diary that showed how far beyond the box and beyond the range of most of his contemporaries he was capable of thinking:

Shall we be caught between a hostile (or at least less friendly) America and a boastful, powerful 'Empire of Charlemagne' – now under French but later bound to be German control? Is this the real reason for 'joining' the Common Market (if we are acceptable) and for abandoning (a) the Seven (b) British agriculture (c) the Commonwealth? It's a grim thought.[4]

Economic considerations were driving in the same direction. The British economy had emerged from the war in better shape than those of the defeated and occupied countries of mainland

Europe. But their recoveries had been far more rapid, so that by 1961 Britain was looking like a flagging pacemaker as younger and fitter rivals swept past it in the race for prosperity. West Germany was doing particularly well. In 1958 both the overall size of its economy and its volume of exports overtook Britain's and, with the start of the new decade, the gap between the two countries was widening. That the country that had lost the war was now so conspicuously winning the peace made a big impression on British public opinion.

Two great problems afflicted the British economy: low productivity and too many strikes. Between 1954 and 1959, unit labour costs were rising twice as fast in Britain than in other industrial countries, and this was reflected in national growth rates. Between 1950 and 1960, West Germany grew by 7.8 per cent, Italy by 5.8 per cent, France by 4.6 per cent, and Britain by 2.7 per cent. A letter that Macmillan wrote to his confidante, Ava Waverley, in August 1960 gives one a feeling for the times: 'We have got through the Power Strike, but the Seamen's Strike is still running: and there are troubles in the Docks and the motor works which threaten us.'[5] This was by no means an untypical situation. A few months later, 1961 opened with the Post Office workers 'working to rule', followed by unofficial strikes in the London Docks, in those days one of the country's biggest ports.

Macmillan and his ministers were not the only people changing their minds about Common Market membership. The Treasury, under its extremely effective permanent secretary, Frank Lee, was deploying its considerable influence on the side of making an application. Leaders of British industry and opinion-formers generally were increasingly coalescing around the view that it might be good for Britain to be linked more closely to the economic winners, and dangerous to be locked out of, or put at a disadvantage, in their markets. The doubts expressed in the 1950s about the ability of the Six to work together, or to achieve anything very much, were giving way to a grudging admiration for what they were achieving, which in turn was influencing the minds of Conservative MPs and some in the constituencies. Europe was gradually beginning to appear in the guise of a vehicle for reversing Britain's economic decline.

The idea, widely canvassed only a few years previously, that the Commonwealth countries could provide more scope for expanding British trade was no longer taken seriously in informed circles. Quite apart from their combined markets being so much smaller than those of Western Europe, they were pursuing policies that were reducing rather than enhancing their attractiveness to Britain. While wanting to retain the privileges conferred by the pre-war Imperial Preference arrangements in selling their agricultural products to Britain, they wanted to lessen their dependence on imports of British manufactured goods by building up industries of their own and widening their range of trading partners.

Once the Cabinet decision had been taken, ministers became engaged in running a highly complex three-ring circus. In one arena, with Heath leading the British team, they were negotiating with the Six. In another, with Macmillan himself the principal point man, they were trying to square those Commonwealth countries – mainly but not only Australia, Canada, and New Zealand – with whom the British people felt a close emotional attachment. In the third, they were trying to convince public opinion that it had become in the country's best interest to join an enterprise from which successive Conservative governments in the 1950s had stood aloof, while making no secret of their belief that it would probably come to nothing.

Whatever the extent to which the facts of Britain's position in the world had changed, and whatever the views of business leaders and informed opinion, this was a U-turn if ever there was one, long before that term had been invented. Moreover, and

Macmillan was very conscious of this, the manifesto on which he had so successfully fought the 1959 election had given no indication that a Conservative government would even consider such a course. A precedent was being set that would become something of a habit of governments in the future, of confronting the electorate with important European initiatives from out of the blue. This was not, or not necessarily, the result of a deliberate decision by ministers. They were driven by events at home and abroad that were beyond their control or that they had not expected to arise, but the result was to create a not-unjustified suspicion in the minds of the electorate that, on European matters, successive governments could not be trusted to speak frankly about their intentions.

Was Macmillan up to the task of convincing the country? The cartoonists of the time loved to portray him as Supermac. His doleful visage and droopy moustache atop a torso clothed in Superman kit made an irresistible image. His achievement in bringing the Conservative Party back from the pits of the humiliation of Suez in 1956 to a third consecutive general election victory in 1959 with an enhanced majority of 100 seats justified the implied superhuman political powers. Labour had expected to win and was flabbergasted by the scale of its defeat.

A leader capable of such a triumph might be capable of anything. But at sixty-six Macmillan was feeling his age. He had been badly wounded on more than one occasion in the First World War and suffered further injuries in a plane crash in the Second. Like many men of his generation, he found that his war wounds continued to cause him pain and weakened his resilience. He was also looking out of date. His rather contrived Edwardian appearance and mannerisms, and photographs of him in plus fours at shooting parties with his wife's ducal relations[6] no longer seemed in tune with contemporary Britain or even the contemporary Conservative Party; they made him an object of mockery. All this was understood by the party's chief whip, Martin Redmayne, who later said that the autumn of 1960 'stands out in my mind as the beginning of the end of the "Supermac" era'.[7]

This was true in terms of the general public, as will become apparent, but it was not true of Macmillan's mastery of the people and machinery of government, which remained extremely effective. In the run up to the crucial 27 July 1961 Cabinet meeting, numerous discussions and ministerial exchanges took place, during which a consensus was created in support of the line he wished the government to take without any dramas or resignations. At the crunch meeting in April 1961, when ministers were asked to state their positions, only Reggie Maudling is on record as having advised against making an application, and he did so on tactical grounds. After reminding his colleagues of how badly their predecessors 'had under-estimated the strength of the forces working for unity between the countries of the Six',[8] he doubted whether an application would be successful. Rab Butler, the most senior member of the Cabinet, concurred with the decision to go ahead while exuding ambivalence, and only fully committed himself at a tête-à-tête dinner with Macmillan in August 1962. Sandys and Soames, while accurately forecasting the objections that would come from the Commonwealth and from British farmers, were strongly in favour.

In the light of the controversies that in the twenty-first century have swirled round the implications for British sovereignty of EU membership, the most significant contribution to the discussion came from the Lord Chancellor, Lord Kilmuir, who, as Sir David Maxwell Fyfe, appeared in Chapter One as one of the architects of the European Convention on Human Rights. In the previous November, Macmillan had advised Heath to seek Kilmuir's advice on the implications for sovereignty if Britain were to join the EEC.

Kilmuir[9] had pulled no punches. He had explained that Parliament would surrender some of its functions to the Council of Ministers, that the Crown's treaty-making powers would be transferred to an international organisation, and that British courts would in some respects be subordinated to the European Court of Justice. As a strong supporter of Britain applying to join the EEC, he urged that these implications should be 'brought out into the open now', because otherwise, 'those who are opposed to the whole idea of joining the Community will certainly seize on them with more damaging effect later on'.[10] At the Cabinet meeting, he repeated this advice and warned his colleagues that 'a major effort of presentation would be needed to persuade the British public to accept these encroachments on national sovereignty'.[11]

Macmillan ignored Kilmuir's advice. In his statement to the House of Commons announcing that the government would be opening negotiations with the Six, in answer to questions and in the debate that took place on 2 and 3 August, he presented the decision in the most prosaic of terms. In a key passage, he said, 'I ask hon. Members to note the word "economic". The Treaty of Rome does not deal with defence. It does not deal with foreign policy. It deals with trade and some of the aspects of human life which are most connected with trade and production'.[12] That statement was in literal terms true, but it entirely disregarded the possibilities inherent in the treaty and what it might lead on to. That he was himself fully aware of how far reaching these possibilities might be is revealed by an exchange he later had with de Gaulle in December 1962. In trying to persuade the general of how much Britain could bring to the European party, one of the attractions he held out was the prospect of a common monetary system.[13]

There was no hint of such possibilities in his initial statement to the House of Commons, his subsequent answers to questions, or the debate on the government's motion to open negotiations. He stressed the commercial advantages and the opportunities for British industry, he undertook to safeguard the interests of the other EFTA member states, he assured the House that nothing would be done that would disadvantage the Commonwealth, and he promised to look after the interests of British agriculture. He referred to the need to resist communist expansion, but not to the kind of worries about the future of East–West relations and how the Western Alliance might evolve that had played such a large part in his own thinking and would do so again in his conversations with de Gaulle.

He could not ignore the sovereignty issue entirely, but he played it down and avoided any mention of the implications for Parliament and the legal system. Instead, he talked about how every treaty involved some diminution of a country's freedom of action and that sovereignty was in reality a matter of degree. In the words of Peter Hennessy, 'This was vintage Macmillan – not exactly dismissive of a crucial question, but skilful in diminishing its rawness or its centrality.'[14] It was also misleading in the sense that it gave the impression that nothing fundamental would change in the British political and legal systems. In taking this approach, he was influenced by the fear expressed in his diary that the issue might split the Conservative Party, as happened in 1846 when the prime minister, Sir Robert Peel, reversed the party's long-standing position by repealing the Corn Laws. That measure was carried on opposition votes, while a venomous Disraeli drove Peel out of the premiership and out of the party. Macmillan had to bear in mind too that the negotiations might fail – he was always aware of this danger – and that the more he built up the importance of the course he had embarked on, the worse such a failure would be for him.

These fears and the presentational decision Macmillan made are perfectly understandable, but they set a precedent for successive governments to be less than honest with the British public about EEC issues and how profound they sometimes were in terms of the national interest or their constitutional implications. From this grew disillusionment and hostility. Kilmuir's prophecy proved to be entirely right. It would have been better in the long run if his advice had been taken, if not by Macmillan, whose application to join failed before it could be put to the British people, then certainly by Heath when he took the country in.

In the short term, Macmillan's tactic paid off. Rumours of what was afoot had, as is generally the case, circulated widely beforehand. A Common Market Committee had been formed by Conservative backbenchers, and an Early Day Motion (a procedural device whereby MPs can get their concerns into the public domain) critical of the government for compromising national sovereignty had been put down and attracted some thirty signatures. However, when it came to the vote on the government motion, fewer than that number abstained. Only one Conservative, Anthony Fell, the member for Yarmouth, voted against the government after describing Macmillan as a 'national disaster' for letting down the Commonwealth.[15] In his diary, Macmillan wrote that 'the Whips have done well', and dismissed the rebels as being 'of two kinds – earnest Imperialists (and) the disgusted group (who oppose the government in every trouble, whatever the subject)'.[16] He was relieved to find no Disraeli or Lord George Bentinck – the upstart Disraeli's aristocratic frontman – among them.

The three leading rebels were Robin Turton, Sir Derek Walker-Smith, and Peter Walker, a disparate trio. Turton, who had been elected to Parliament in 1929 aged twenty-five, was an aristocratic Yorkshire landowner, while Walker-Smith, who had been elected in 1945, was a QC with the most pretentious style of oratory I have ever heard. Both were former ministers of health,

an office which in those days was outside the Cabinet. Their ministerial careers were clearly over, in Walker-Smith's case crowned
by the award of a baronetcy in 1960. Peter Walker was a man of a
very different stripe. He had only entered the House a short time
before, as a result of a by-election in March 1961. At the age of
twenty-nine, he was a former chair of the Young Conservatives,
in those days an important organisation within the party, for
which he had been awarded an MBE. He was also already well
known in financial circles in the City, where he was carving out
a name for himself in the rapidly expanding unit trust sector.
In due course he would become a close ally of Heath, in whose
Cabinet he served from 1970 to 1974. Subsequently he also
served in Margaret Thatcher's, despite frequently being at odds
with her.

Two names stand out for their absence. Both were lulled, or
chose to be lulled, by the way Macmillan had presented his case.
One is Thatcher herself, who had entered Parliament in the 1959
election. She was already committed to the pro-entry side of the
argument as a member of the European Union of Women, an
organisation founded some years earlier to promote European
integration. Both as a member of that body's Judicial Panel and
as a barrister, she could not have been unaware of at least some
of the sovereignty implications of the Treaty of Rome and she
must have understood the substance of the rebels' argument. But,
as she puts it in her autobiography, 'I saw the EEC as essentially a
trading framework – a Common Market – and neither shared nor
took very seriously the idealistic rhetoric with which "Europe"
was already being dressed in some quarters.'[17] In this she was
typical of most of her Parliamentary colleagues. She was also on
the verge of her first ministerial office and not likely to do anything to prejudice her chances. The following October, she was
appointed parliamentary secretary at the Ministry of Pensions.

The other notable absentee was Enoch Powell, who had stood

out against the ECSC ten years earlier, because of its implications for eventual political union. In 1961 he was minister of health, and so had not taken part in the Cabinet's private debates. As he later explained, he saw the matter at that time exclusively in terms of free trade and increasing the volume of trade, and did not grasp the political implications of membership until some years later.[18] If a man of his outstanding intelligence could have made such a mistake, it is hardly surprising that so many other Members of Parliament should have done so as well.

With Lord Beaverbrook's *Daily Express*, in those days a newspaper with a huge circulation and a force to be reckoned with in Conservative circles, campaigning vigorously against British membership of the EEC, Macmillan worried about what might happen at the Party conference in Brighton in October. Forty-two motions were submitted for debate on the Europe issue; some, like that from Walker's Worcester constituency, were hostile to the government. It was feared that a grassroots revolt might occur, but all went well. Only some thirty or forty delegates out of the 4,000 who attended voted against the official line, although this certainly understated the level of unease in the conference hall. In his closing speech, after all the business had been concluded, Macmillan presented Britain joining the EEC as creating a common economic front in Europe to match that of NATO in defence. He also warned that it would be like a cold shower for industry.

With the party in Parliament and the country behind it, the government could get on with squaring the Commonwealth and negotiating with the Six. At the same time, it had to tackle a difficult domestic agenda. Inflation and unemployment were both rising, the trade gap and the budget deficit were both widening, and there was growing concern in some provincial cities and parts of London about the increasing numbers of immigrants arriving from the West Indies and the Indian subcontinent.

It was, however, in Macmillan's own political backyard that a bombshell exploded in March 1962. In Orpington, not far from his own constituency of Bromley, Eric Lubbock won the most sensational by-election since the war by transforming a Conservative majority of 15,000 into a Liberal one of 8,000. Nothing remotely like it had been seen before.

The party chair, Iain Macleod, himself among the most charismatic and perceptive politicians of that period, conducted a post-mortem and reported that dissatisfaction with the government's economic policy was the key. Shortly afterwards, the chancellor of the exchequer, Selwyn Lloyd, made matters worse when he mismanaged the introduction of a new policy to restrain wage increases. Further by-election setbacks then followed.

Macmillan felt himself to be under siege on two fronts – on the one side, by middle-class voters in places like Orpington who believed their living standards were being held back while the wages of the industrial working class were moving ahead, and, on the other, by right-wingers in the party who had always disliked him, led by Lord Salisbury. He decided to play that traditional card of a prime minister in trouble: a reshuffle to bring in new faces and get rid of old ones, notably the unfortunate Lloyd. But instead of conducting it in an orderly fashion to show that he was in command of events, he panicked. On what became famous as the Night of the Long Knives of 13 July 1962, he sacked seven of his twenty-one Cabinet ministers, a misjudgement from which his reputation never recovered. The future Liberal leader Jeremy Thorpe captured, and helped to form, the mood of the moment with his celebrated quip: 'Greater love hath no man than this, that he lay down his friends for his life.'[19] Kilmuir was among the casualties.

Besides these conventional political problems, Macmillan was in trouble from an entirely new phenomenon. 1962 was the year when the satirists captured the public's attention and played an important role in shaping attitudes towards politicians and those in authority. The television programme *That Was the Week that Was*, commonly known as *TW3*, commanded huge audiences every Saturday evening with its mockery of the pomposities and pretensions of the political establishment and those in authority. Macmillan, with his stylised and dated gestures and manner of speaking, was their favourite target. Several members of its cast went on to have successful careers in show business. One, Ian Lang, turned to Conservative politics and in the 1990s became a senior member of John Major's Cabinet.[20] The programme's impact was reinforced by the satirical news magazine *Private Eye*, founded the year before, and on the London stage by the comedy review *Beyond the Fringe*. Their combined influence on the public mood was tremendous and very much to the detriment of Macmillan and all that he appeared to stand for.

Party chair Macleod believed that if only the EEC negotiations could be brought to a successful conclusion, they would provide the country with the psychological fillip and the new role that it needed. In April he told his Enfield constituency association that 'Britain ought to play her full part in the great movement towards European unity. We are convinced it is right for ourselves and for the Commonwealth, which needs a strong, prosperous Britain with money to invest overseas ... we should thrill to the challenge.'[21] If the government could have mounted a self-confident campaign along these lines it might have been able to galvanise its supporters and revive its fortunes, but it could not do so while the outcome of the negotiations remained uncertain.

To add to the difficulty, Europe was continuing to divide the party. In the House of Commons, several young MPs, including the future Cabinet minister Jim Prior, the world-famous athlete Christopher Chataway, and two men who would in later years become well known anti-Europeans, Nick Ridley and John

Biffen, had formed themselves into an unofficial support group for Heath. In June, another backbencher, Dudley Smith, had reported to Heath that 189 of his colleagues were in favour of entry and 77 opposed. In the same month, the Labour MP and future Cabinet minister Dick Crossman recorded in his diary that Sir Derek Walker-Smith and Peter Walker were claiming to have the sympathy of sixty fellow Conservatives for a pamphlet they had published entitled *A Call to the Commonwealth*, which presented an alternative to the EEC.[22]

In the constituencies, Conservative agents were expressing their concern over the activities of the Anti-Common Market League. The opinion polls fluctuated on a downward trend from a peak of 53 per cent in favour of entry in December 1961 to 47 per cent in May 1962 and thereafter to below 40 per cent with a large proportion of Don't Knows. When the party conference took place at Llandudno in October, the government again carried the day with much the same overwhelming majority as in the previous year. Such majorities in support of the leadership were the norm at Conservative conferences in those days and did not necessarily reflect firmly held opinions among the delegates.

The real drama had taken place the week before at the Labour Party conference in Brighton, where the party's leader, Hugh Gaitskell, had made the most famous speech of his life. He had given the impression beforehand that in the end his view on whether Britain should enter the EEC would depend on the terms of any proposed accession agreement. In Brighton, in passages of great eloquence, he put the issue into an altogether different context by dwelling on the implications of federalism and political union. Britain's position in a federation, he argued, would be like that of Western Australia or New South Wales: 'We should be like them. This is what it means; it does mean the end of Britain as an independent nation state.'[23] To drive home his argument, he then uttered the phrase about 'the end of a thousand years of history' for which he will always be remembered. The whole tenor of his speech was hostile to entry, but he was careful not to rule it out entirely if the interests of the Commonwealth could be safeguarded.

Macmillan had understood from the moment he took the decision to apply to join the EEC that he had to square the Commonwealth, by which he meant primarily Australia, Canada, and New Zealand. If their prime ministers were to appeal over his head to the British people, his task would be made immeasurably more difficult. The newly independent members in Asia and Africa enjoyed goodwill and sympathy in the Labour Party, but among Conservatives it was the old white Commonwealth countries that counted. Their desire to play an increasingly distinctive role on the world stage and the extent to which the diversification of their trade was weakening their economic links with Britain had not at that time weakened their emotional hold on British public opinion, based, as it was, on history, the shared wartime experience, and family connections. The Australian prime minister, Bob Menzies, was widely regarded as the key figure. With the prestige derived from having held that position during the war, he had, in Macmillan's opinion, 'the power to prevent Britain joining Europe'.[24]

In order to ensure that their interests would be fully taken into account before any final settlement with the EEC was reached, the British government had promised that a Commonwealth conference would be held. It took place in September 1962, lasted two weeks, and involved a good deal of hard bargaining and harsh words from the leaders of both the old and the new Commonwealth. The Canadian prime minister, John Diefenbaker, turned out to be particularly difficult, but at one time or another Macmillan confided complaints about all of them, including Menzies, to his diary. As the end approached, he feared that more than one communiqué might be issued, thereby revealing the extent of the Commonwealth unease. That disaster was avoided, but it was obvious from the final text that he had secured no more than a reluctant acquiescence that the EEC negotiations should continue. Gaitskell argued that it showed that the terms so far negotiated would have to be improved upon. If agreement had been reached with the Six, it is hard to see how another Commonwealth meeting could have been avoided.

The demands made by the Commonwealth leaders showed how little they understood the weakness of Britain's negotiating position. In the 1950s, when the ECSC and the EEC were being formed, the Six actively wanted British participation. Now the British were mendicants asking to be let in. In his autobiography, Heath writes that Monnet advised him that the best way to overcome this problem was to forget about negotiating, to sign up immediately, and then, as insiders, to 'seek adjustments of the Community's institutions and policies to meet our own particular needs'.[25] British public opinion would have found such an apparent surrender hard to understand, to put it mildly, and the Commonwealth would have been up in arms, but, as Heath recognised, it 'was a tempting proposal'.[26] The Six had not yet established much in the way of common policies. If Britain had come straight in, it could have taken part in their formation, with the Common Agricultural Policy (CAP) top of the agenda.

For precisely that reason, de Gaulle would never have countenanced such a proposal. British historians have endlessly analysed the discussions that took place between Macmillan and de Gaulle while the negotiations were in progress in an effort to penetrate the opaque oratory, high flown strategic considerations, and lessons of history with which the general clothed his arguments. There has been equally endless analysis of the impact on his reasoning of the Nassau Agreement in December 1962 between Macmillan and President Kennedy, under the terms of which Britain agreed to buy Polaris missiles for its nuclear

submarine fleet: a deal that underscored both its nuclear dependence on and close relationship with the United States.

Reading Macmillan's own account of his talks with de
Gaulle, the single most surprising point to emerge in the light
of subsequent history is his effort, mentioned above, to tempt
the general with the prospect of 'a common monetary system'.
Had the general been interested, where might it have led? His
most influential economic adviser was Jacques Rueff, who is
credited with saying 'Europe shall be made through the currency or it shall not be made'.[27] Might Britain and France, rather
than France and Germany, have led the way towards Economic
and Monetary Union (EMU)? It is one of history's tantalising
what-might-have-beens.

Undoubtedly de Gaulle wished it to be thought that his rejection was based on Britain's unsuitability for membership of a
continental European club owing to its different history, its international links, its closeness to the United States, and its own
particular outlook on the world. No doubt these considerations
lay behind his veto up to a point. But there were others as well
that would not have sounded so sonorous or impressive at the
carefully staged press conference, amounting almost to a state
occasion, at which he delivered his verdict on 14 January 1963. It
will be recalled from Chapter One that in 1946 he had held a very
different view. When Churchill had sought his opinion on his
Zurich speech, de Gaulle had replied that if ever France was to
be won over to the idea of European union, it would have to be
in partnership with Britain, and that their two countries would
have to adopt the same approach towards Germany.

Why, then, had he changed his opinion? Not the least of the
general's strengths was his adaptability to changing circumstances. He had changed his mind because of the formation of
the EEC without Britain. He had no love for the EEC as such.
It was too supranational for his taste, and the Commission had

too big a role. He would try unsuccessfully to change both these characteristics. To set against these blemishes, it offered two advantages that he was determined to exploit to the maximum. It enabled France to act as West Germany's patron on its long march back to respectability after the war, and, in alliance with West Germany, it enabled France to ensure that the EEC would adopt policies in line with French interests.

As Robert Marjolin, the French vice-president of the newly formed Commission, later explained in his autobiography, in policy terms this meant first and foremost the CAP: 'I was convinced that if there was no agreement on a common agricultural policy, France would pull out of the Common Market.'[28] If France pulled out, the whole edifice would have collapsed. For West Germany, which saw the Common Market as the means by which to recover its international standing and to rebuild its economic strength within a framework that would not alarm its neighbours, this would have been a catastrophe. It would have liked Britain to join and hoped that in due course it would, but not at the expense of its relationship with France. Again, to quote Marjolin, 'The Europe that was being constructed in these first years of the sixties was essentially a Franco-German Europe',[29] which applied to other polices as well as to the CAP.

The other four member states were content to go along with this. Belgium, the Netherlands, and Luxembourg attached the greatest importance to the reconciliation of France and Germany while benefiting from the CAP and other policies. In fact, the principal architect of the CAP had been the Dutch commissioner, Sicco Mansholt. Italy was in a somewhat special position, wracked by chronic political instability and with a large communist party. Its political class saw membership of the EEC as underpinning the country's fragile democracy and as an anchor that kept it within the mainstream of Western European political society. It, too, gained greatly from the CAP. All four countries regretted that Britain had stood aside from the EEC in the 1950s and looked forward to it one day becoming a member, but not if that meant disrupting the arrangements they were putting together, and certainly not if it meant upsetting France, which they regarded as the lynchpin of the whole enterprise.

The way the system worked, and why France did not want Britain to join the EEC at that time, was frankly explained to Christopher Soames by his French opposite number, Edgard Pisani, in a conversation Soames reported back to Macmillan, who recorded it in French: '*Mon cher. C'est très simple. Maintenant, avec les six, il y a cinq poules et un coq. Si vous joignez avec des autres pays, il y aura peut-être sept ou huit poules. Mais il y aura deux coqs. Alors – ce n'est pas aussi agréable.*'[30] The reference to other countries reflects the widespread assumption that, if Britain's application were successful, Ireland, Denmark, and Norway would have joined with it.

When the guillotine fell on his hopes of leading Britain into the EEC, Macmillan had the stuffing knocked out of him both politically and personally. The government's credibility was further damaged two months later by the eruption of the Profumo scandal, linking Jack Profumo, the secretary of state for war, with the call girls Christine Keeler and Mandy Rice-Davies, who in turn were linked to an attaché at the Soviet embassy. Macmillan, looking increasingly forlorn and out of touch, held on against mounting odds until, on 8 October 1963, he was taken into the King Edward VII Hospital suffering from a prostate condition. From there, he deployed his influence to ensure that the succession should go to Douglas-Home rather than Butler. In normal circumstances, Macmillan would have gone to Buckingham Palace to advise the Queen that Lord Home was the man she should call on to form a government. As he was unable do that, he could have submitted the advice in writing. Instead, the Queen took the unprecedented step of coming to his bedside, so that he could proffer the advice in person. Lord Home then renounced his peerage and, as Sir Alec Douglas-Home, was returned to Parliament at a by-election.

Badly though they had ended, the negotiations were the making of Heath. Before being put in charge of them, he was best known as the chief whip who had held the party together throughout all the turmoil and anger generated by the Suez debacle, and the subsequent change of leadership: a formidable achievement, but of a distinctly backroom nature. The negotiations made him a household name. He was widely believed to have performed magnificently and, from that moment on, was regarded as one of the most promising of the younger generation of Conservative ministers, if not quite on a par with Maudling and MacLeod. His reputation was also high in the capitals of the Six, including with de Gaulle. When the two men met in 1965, de Gaulle told him, 'If you become prime minister, you will be the man who will lead Britain into the European Community,'[31] a statement that gives credence to the view that his own objection to Britain joining in 1963 was one of timing, while the foundations of the EEC were being laid, rather than principle. They continued to keep in touch and, two days after the general died in November 1970, Heath received a warmly inscribed copy of the last volume of his memoirs. A few months earlier, in June of that year, he had become prime minister and was preparing to fulfil the general's prophecy.

3

Heath's Triumph and Tragedy 1963–1975

Politics has sometimes been described as the art of the possible. And sometimes in politics everything falls into place so that what was impossible only a short time before becomes possible. Such was the case with Heath fulfilling de Gaulle's prophecy that he would lead Britain into the EEC.

Four things had to happen. Heath had to become leader of the Conservative Party, and to lead his party to victory in a general election. British public opinion had to move sufficiently in favour of joining, or at least be sufficiently acquiescent for his government to carry the necessary legislation through Parliament. Finally, with de Gaulle gone, the Six had to be sufficiently open to the idea of Britain becoming a member to enable a successful negotiation to take place. Between 14 January 1963, when the general's veto was announced, and 1 January 1973, when Britain became a member, everything fell into place.

The simplest step turned out to be the first. Alec Douglas-Home delayed calling a general election until 15 October 1964, which Labour then won by the narrowest of margins: an overall majority of only four. In the circumstances, and after thirteen years of Conservative rule, this was a considerable personal triumph for the widely underestimated Douglas-Home. Nonetheless it was a defeat and one that would obviously have to be followed by another election, at which the new prime minister, Harold Wilson, would seek to increase his majority. When it became clear that this would not take place in 1965, Douglas-Home announced his intention to resign on 22 July of that year. The informal and mysterious process by which he had become party leader had been severely criticised as old fashioned and inappropriate for the second half of the twentieth century. As a result, a new system had been instituted – a secret ballot of Conservative MPs with the requirement that to win on the first ballot, a candidate had to secure an overall majority plus a margin of 15 per cent of those voting.

Polling day was scheduled for the 27th, thereby allowing minimal time for open campaigning, although behind the scenes positioning and lobbying had been taking place for some time with the former opponent of EEC entry, Peter Walker, running a very effective operation on Heath's behalf.

Europe was not a point of contention any more than it had been at the general election. For the moment it was a dead issue. The overriding concern of most Conservative MPs was to find the candidate least like the old-fashioned, upper-class, tweedy images of Macmillan and Douglas-Home and best able to tackle Wilson. With his reassuring northern accent and the fatherly pipe he habitually smoked in public on the one hand, and his economics expertise and talk of 'the white hot heat of the technological revolution' on the other, Wilson came across as both a man of the people and a professional executive, a combination ideally suited to the mood of Britain in the 1960s.

When the Conservatives went into opposition, the favourite to become leader had been the former chancellor of the exchequer and de facto deputy leader, Reggie Maudling. As time passed, it became increasingly apparent that, for all his considerable ability and charm, he was irredeemably lazy. By contrast Heath, now shadow chancellor, was winning plaudits for the formidable energy, attention to detail, and forensic skill with which he was opposing the government's Finance Bill and confounding his opposite number, Jim Callaghan. Michael Jopling, who had entered the Commons in the 1964 election, recalls that this persuaded him and others of the 1959 and 1964 vintages to support Heath,[1] as did some of the ablest of the younger former ministers, including Thatcher and Sir Keith Joseph. If Iain MacLeod, who had an enthusiastic following among younger and more left-wing Conservatives, of whom I was one, and was a close friend of Maudling, had stood, he would probably have attracted enough votes away from Heath to give Maudling victory. His decision not to do so and to vote for Heath handed victory to the latter.

When the result of the first ballot was announced, Heath had 150 votes to Maudling's 133 with Enoch Powell trailing on 15. This meant that Maudling, who had expected to win, could have gone through to a second ballot, but within an hour he telephoned Walker to concede. 'What is there left for me to do save sit here and get pissed?' he told his Cabinet colleague, Edward Boyle, in the Commons Smoking Room.[2] Powell, who was putting down a marker for the future rather than expecting to win, was disappointed by the numbers, but pleased with the impact he had made.

Although Europe did not feature in this leadership election, the result was crucial in determining Britain's European future. Maudling had always been a doubter about membership of the EEC. Whether, if he had become prime minister, he would have been convinced by the arguments that persuaded Wilson in 1967 to reverse his previous position and to apply for membership is impossible to say. What is certain is that he would never have committed himself so single-mindedly and at almost any cost to bringing the negotiations with the Six to a successful conclusion, as Heath was later to do.

This was not simply a matter of character. Heath's devotion to the European cause had very deep roots. Before the war, he had travelled in Spain during the civil war and, unlike most

Conservatives, supported the Republic against Franco. He had also travelled in Nazi Germany, where he had attended one of Hitler's infamous Nuremberg rallies and been appalled by the nature of the regime. After wartime service in the Royal Artillery in which he rose to the rank of Lieutenant-Colonel (Powell rose even higher to Brigadier), he had witnessed at first hand the devastation wrought on Germany by the Allied bombing.

To a degree that was extremely rare among his British contemporaries, Heath shared the dream of men like Monnet and Spaak of building, by means of the EEC, a European edifice that would make war impossible among Europeans and safeguard democracy against fascism as well as communism. He wanted Britain to be part of that edifice and saw it as a means by which British influence in Europe and the world could be increased, just as French leaders saw it as a vehicle for extending French influence. Though a good friend of the United States, he was untouched by the self-delusion and sentimentality with which other British prime ministers tended to view 'the special relationship'. He believed that Britain's strongest foreign policy relationship should be with the EEC and its members. In domestic politics he saw EEC membership and the economic opportunities that went with it as an integral part of his programme for modernising Britain.

In the first statement of policy issued under his leadership, he made his intentions clear: 'When the present difficulties and uncertainties in Europe are resolved, we believe it would be right to take the first favourable opportunity to join the Community and to assist others who wish, in the Commonwealth and EFTA, to seek closer association with it.'[3]

When making this pledge, Heath knew, and the party knew, that he had no hope of delivering on it for some years to come. It was universally expected that whenever Wilson chose to call another election the country would confirm its 1964 decision by giving him the increased majority he needed. In March 1966 it duly did so, returning Labour with an overall majority of ninety-eight. Thereafter, Heath's role was to settle in for a whole Parliament of opposition and to prepare for a do-or-die bid for the premiership in 1970 or 1971. He would, he knew, be out if he lost again.

During those years, Europe was by no means the most divisive issue within the Conservative Party. Rhodesia's Unilateral Declaration of Independence and the racial tensions following Commonwealth immigration into Britain aroused stronger feelings. In November 1965, the white minority government of Rhodesia (now Zimbabwe), having refused to cooperate with the British government's plans to transfer power to the black majority, declared itself independent. The British government responded by imposing sanctions and seeking to isolate it from the international community, a decision that split the Conservative Party at every level. Heath tried to bridge the divide by instructing the party to abstain on a key vote to impose oil sanctions, only to find eighty-one of his followers going their own way – fifty opposing sanctions and thirty-one supporting them. In the constituencies, support for the rebel regime – 'our kith and kin' – was overwhelming. The row rumbled on throughout Heath's time in office, undermining his position with the right wing of the party.

The other question was even more explosive. In the 1964 election, the Conservative candidate in the Midlands constituency of Smethwick had won the seat from Labour on an overtly racist platform, thereby encouraging those in the party who believed race would be an election-winner. Within the Shadow Cabinet, Powell, who also had a Midlands constituency in Wolverhampton, became the spokesman for all those, whatever their party, who saw immigration as a threat to their national identity. This put Heath and his other colleagues in an awkward position.

They agreed with Powell that immigration must be curbed and were aware of his popularity throughout the country. At the same time, they deplored the racist tone of his message. The principal opponent of the Powell approach was MacLeod, now shadow chancellor, one of whose supporters, the maverick left-wing MP Humphry Berkeley, actually left the Conservative Party in protest at Powell's activities.

In April 1968 Powell brought matters to a head with an apocalyptic speech in Birmingham in which he quoted the Sybil's prophecy from Virgil's *Aeneid*[4] that she would see terrible wars and 'the Tiber foaming with much blood'.[5] Heath was outraged at what he saw as a deliberate attempt to encourage racial prejudice and sacked Powell. The immediate result was a flood of support for Powell. Eleven constituency associations in the south of England came out in support of him and of the 2,756 letters received by the leader of the opposition's office, only twelve approved of Heath's action. Thereafter, Powell spoke out on a number of other issues that put him increasingly at odds with the party leadership, and a few months before the 1970 election added opposition to entering the EEC to the list.

Meanwhile, Heath sought to mobilise the party behind an ambitious programme for the modernisation of Britain. The aim was to transform the country's economic performance by de-regulating industry, curbing inflation, reforming industrial relations, and re-structuring the machinery of government. He and his supporters regarded joining the EEC as an integral part of this programme. Numerous policy groups involving MPs and outside experts were set up. Their purpose was partly to devise policies for specific sectors (I was on one dealing with the state-owned industries, chaired by Nicholas Ridley), and partly to create a sense of common purpose and shared endeavour. At the heart of the process was the work on the machinery of government known as the New Style of Government programme, in which Heath took a deep personal interest and was assisted by two young men, who these days would be called special advisers: the future Cabinet minister David Howell, and Mark Schreiber.[6]

The two advisers ranged across the whole landscape of government and drew on ideas from wherever they could find them. Yet, as Howell later recalled, the implications of joining the EEC 'hardly impinged on our deliberations'.[7] They looked across the Atlantic to Washington and the great American think tanks for ideas, but they did not ask the governments of the Six how they were adjusting their practices to cope with their membership of the EEC. They did not consider Kilmuir's warning about how the legal framework within which Britain was governed would be altered by membership, nor did they look at the implications for Whitehall and Westminster of decisions taken in Brussels. These were less far-reaching in the 1960s than they later became, but that they would become increasingly significant was implicit in the Treaty of Rome. That Heath of all men should apparently have been so neglectful of what his great project involved for the future governance of Britain is extraordinary. It is no wonder that so many others failed to appreciate it, only to be shocked when reality caught up with them after entry.

While Heath prepared for the future, Wilson grappled with the present. Britain's economic performance continued to fall behind that of other comparable countries, inflation remained intractable, and, despite the Labour Party's links with the trade unions, industrial relations worsened. The government's inability to bring down the Rhodesian regime created difficulties with the new Commonwealth countries, while the Vietnam War, which Wilson wisely kept Britain out of, strained relations with the United States. The decision on financial grounds to run down the British military presence east of Suez emphasised the extent to which the country was ceasing to be a global power and becoming a purely European one.

Like Macmillan before him, Wilson began to see British entry into the EEC as a way out of the country's economic problems and the means by which it could find a new role in the world. On 19 February 1966 Dick Crossman, now a Cabinet minister, noted in his diary, 'As he [Wilson] sees it, the difficulties of staying outside Europe and surviving as an independent power are very great compared with entering on the right conditions.'[8] Once he had increased his Parliamentary majority in the March 1966 general election, Wilson began to overcome the divisions within his Cabinet and to prepare the way among the Six with what he called a 'probe' before officially launching an application in May 1967.

Heath regarded entry into the EEC as a matter of such importance that he had no hesitation in supporting Wilson's move. Despite warnings of a split in the party by his chief whip, Willie Whitelaw, and consternation in the 1922 Committee at such an unusual procedure, he imposed a three-line whip in support of the government's policy. It was approved by an overwhelming majority of 488 to 62 with 26 Conservatives voting against, including 6 Ulster Unionists who, in those days, took the Conservative whip, and 34 Labour MPs. Significant numbers from both parties abstained. Among those voting for entry was Powell, the last occasion on which he would do so.

Because Wilson's application never looked like succeeding and was again vetoed by de Gaulle in November, only six months after its launch, its significance is often overlooked. In fact, it was an important step on the road towards Britain's entry into the EEC. As Hugo Young explains in *This Blessed Plot*, 'The second try assembled, for the first time, a critical mass of support among the political class for the proposition that Britain should become a European country. The government was committed, the opposition agreed, the moving powers in business were desperate, and the people did not dissent.'[9] The mandarins in the Foreign Office were also strongly in favour. Within the Conservative Party the issue was, for the moment, quiescent.

Wilson was not put off by the veto and planned to re-launch his application as soon as de Gaulle left office, which eventually occurred in April 1969. When he called a general election for 18 June 1970, he had already arranged that the new application would be formally delivered on 30 June, and the officials and plans were in place to get the negotiations off to a flying start.

So, both the Conservatives and Labour went into the election with manifesto commitments to open negotiations with the EEC. Labour's were the more ambitious, with a clear statement of intent:

> We have applied for membership of the EEC and negotiations are due to start in a few weeks' time. They will be pressed with determination with the purpose of joining an enlarged community provided that British and Commonwealth interests can be safeguarded.[10]

The Conservative commitment was more hedged about. The relevant passage read:

> If we can negotiate the right terms, we believe it would be in the long-term interest of the British people for Britain to join the European Economic Community, and that it would make a major contribution to both the prosperity and security of our country. The opportunities are immense. Economic growth and a higher standard of living would result from having a larger market.[11]

It went on to say that 'our sole commitment is to negotiate; no more no less', and concluded with an assurance that 'ministers and members will listen to the views of their constituents and have in mind, as is natural and legitimate, primarily the effect of entry upon the standard of living of the individual citizens whom they represent'. There was no mention of constitutional implications. Kilmuir, who had died in 1967, would have been disappointed to see that the advice he had given ten years previously to be frank with the British people about the implications of EEC membership for Parliament and the courts was once again being comprehensively rejected.

On election night, the first constituency to declare was Guildford, where David Howell increased the Conservative majority with a 5.3 per cent swing: more than enough, if replicated across the country, to ensure a Conservative government. The nation was flabbergasted. The overwhelming expectation had been that Labour would cruise to victory. So sure were the TV pundits that in Smith Square, where the two major parties' headquarters were situated, the cameras were all at Labour's Transport House with none at Conservative Central Office. 'In a fraction of a second,' the Labour Cabinet minister, Tony Benn, recorded in his diary, 'one went from pretty confident expectation of victory to absolute certainty of defeat. It was a quite remarkable experience.'[12]

Throughout the campaign, the polls had signalled a Labour victory. As late as 12 June, six days before polling day, NOP put Labour 12.4 points ahead and the bookies were offering 20/1 against a Conservative victory. Those of us who were standing as Conservative candidates – I was in the safe seat of the Cities of London and Westminster – were perplexed. What we were experiencing on the ground seemed so different. However, instead of doubting the polls, most of us either assumed that our local circumstances deviated from the national norm or that we must be missing something.

Sara Morrison, for many years Heath's closest female friend and adviser in an entirely non-romantic way, recalls that throughout the campaign he and his team 'believed that we could/would win and stayed deaf to all else'.[13] The future foreign secretary Douglas Hurd, then in charge of Heath's private office, paints a less sanguine picture in his memoir *An End to Promises*.[14] As the campaign approached the end, the press was full of speculation as to who Heath's successor would be, with Powell and Whitelaw frequently mentioned. Heath records that on polling day itself, Lord Carrington, the shadow defence minister, told him 'that should we lose, I would be expected immediately to stand down'.[15] Heath replied that that was his intention.

Hurd rejoiced that 'the experts, the know-alls and the trend setters had been confounded'.[16] He attributed the outcome, at least in part, to Heath's personal preface to the manifesto promising a new style of modern and straightforward government, coupled with the widespread public distrust of Wilson's reputation for trickery and sharp practice. The public's fear of rising prices and Labour's inability to get inflation under control plus doubts about its economic management were certainly important factors. So, too, was the support of Powell, who, with an eye to a leadership contest if Heath lost, urged his followers, both within the party and outside, to vote Conservative. His stature in the country had become so great that during the campaign the Press Association had assigned two reporters to cover his activities, against one each for Wilson and Heath. His endorsement was correspondingly important. Had he stood for the leadership after a Conservative defeat at the general election, he would have been hard to beat, a frightening prospect for men like Carrington, Whitelaw, and Macleod, as well as for many others.

Whatever the reasons, Europe and the question of whether and on what terms Britain should enter the EEC barely featured in the campaign. With both major parties in favour of joining, it played no part in determining the outcome.

A month after taking office, the new government suffered a body blow from which it never recovered. Macleod's death on

20 July removed the colleague whose gifts and qualities Heath most needed. Heath's great weakness as a national leader who wanted to bring about change was his frequent inability to convey a vision or excite an audience. Sometimes he was able to do so, but too often a habitual woodenness stood in the way.

Macleod, by contrast, was a spellbinding orator with the capacity to move people with the power of his ideas. Had he lived, he might have been able to persuade the British people of the EEC's potential to provide Britain with a new role in the world as well as greater economic opportunities. At the very least, he would have conveyed a sense of excitement and of a new beginning. In the words of his biographer and close friend Nigel Fisher, himself a Conservative MP, 'We should certainly have joined the European Community with greater public enthusiasm and excitement if Macleod had lived to put the case for doing so.'[17]

Significantly, Macleod, with the support of Sir Ian Gilmour, another enthusiast for entry, had argued through the spring of 1970 in favour of holding a referendum before the country finally joined as the best means of securing the popular consent required for such a historic decision. In May, in a speech in Paris about the enlargement of the EEC, Heath had declared that it would require 'the full-hearted consent of the Parliaments and peoples' of new member countries in order for them to join.[18] Hurd, who was present at the occasion and probably drafted the speech, later said that when Heath uttered these words, there was no thought in his mind of a referendum.[19]

They were, however, widely interpreted as implying that there should be one, and Heath was accused of bad faith when he rejected proposals to hold one. Opponents of entry, such as Powell and Neil Marten on the Conservative side, and Labour's Douglas Jay and Benn, argued that such a major constitutional innovation required a direct mandate from the people. Heath countered with the argument that the will of the people would be expressed through Parliament. He further argued that the EEC would not take the British negotiators seriously if it was known that they might subsequently be disavowed by their own electorate. The three other countries that simultaneously negotiated entry alongside Britain – Ireland, Denmark, and Norway – all held referendums after the negotiations had been completed. The Irish and Danes voted Yes. The Norwegians, to everyone's surprise, voted No out of a mixture of dislike of the recently introduced Common Fisheries Policy and worries about sovereignty.

Heath was right that a commitment to a referendum would have complicated the negotiations. It would certainly have constituted an additional hurdle to be surmounted before Britain could fulfil his ambition to join. His biographer Philip Ziegler wonders whether he feared that 'a referendum with Labour quite possibly against acceptance and Enoch Powell leading the anti-marketeers in a rampage for rejection'[20] would have de-railed the project. Against that, it is at the very least arguable that the knowledge that the electorate would have the final say might have enabled the British negotiators to secure better terms. What is, I think, undeniable is that had there been a referendum, had Macleod lived to take part in it, and had the British people voted to join, they would have entered the EEC with a deeper sense of commitment than in the event they did.

The fact that Europe had not featured in the election did not mean that the general public was relaxed about it. As opinion among the leaders of business and industry hardened in favour of joining the EEC, popular opinion began moving against. While de Gaulle's veto of his application had encouraged Wilson to redouble his efforts to join, it had strengthened the opposition of others to the whole project. Neil Marten spoke for many when he said, 'We have been rebuffed twice and really cannot continue to live in this uncertainty ... Now we must press on on our own and look for new alternatives.'[21] The eloquence of Powell's ceaseless diatribes as the EEC took over from immigration as his principal theme were also having an effect.

Another factor was a government White Paper, published before the election in February 1970, warning that the cost of food could rise by up to 25 per cent and the cost of living by up to 5 per cent with a further hit to the balance of payments. These figures were the result of a decision by the EEC in December 1969 to stop financing the Community budget by national contributions and to replace them by a system known as 'own resources', in which all customs duties and levies arising from trade between member states and non-member states would belong as of right to the EEC rather than to the member states that collected them. To this would be added a levy, determined each year in the annual budget, of up to 1 per cent of their VAT proceeds. As the CAP accounted for the lion's share of the budget's expenditure, this meant that countries whose agricultural sector was a large proportion of their total economy, like France, would gain at the expense of those in the reverse position, like Britain.

A less determined incoming prime minister than Heath might at this point have pressed the pause button on the Europe project. Besides having to tackle Britain's perennial economic problems, the government was committed to a highly contentious bill to reform industrial relations by making it more difficult to call strikes. In addition, it was faced with a worsening crisis in Northern Ireland. The Troubles, involving violence between the Catholic and Protestant communities, had broken out two years earlier, and British troops were having to be deployed in ever larger numbers. But retreat was not Heath's way. He determined to press on with getting into the EEC as quickly as possible.

On 30 June, the date on which Wilson had planned for his proposed minister for Europe, George Thomson, to present Britain's formal application at a meeting of the EEC Council of Ministers in Luxembourg, Heath's nominee, Anthony Barber, turned up in his stead. It was to be his only meeting. On MacLeod's death, he was promoted to chancellor of the exchequer, and Geoffrey Rippon took over the portfolio. The chief official negotiator was Sir Con O'Neill, who had been one of Heath's principal lieutenants during the negotiations over the Macmillan application and subsequently went on to write the official history of the negotiations that took place between 1970 and 1972.

The caveats and cautious wording about Europe in the Conservative election manifesto were swept aside when it came to the negotiations. As O'Neill was later to explain in the official history, 'What mattered was to get into the Community, and thereby restore our position at the centre of European affairs which, since 1958, we had lost.'[22] This meant that in practice the scope for the British negotiators was extremely limited. Since 1961 the EEC had created an enormous body of laws, rules, and precedents, known in the jargon as the *acquis communautaire*. All were the result of detailed and complex negotiations, trade-offs, and compromises on the part of the six original members. Some went back a long way. Others were very recent, notably the Common Fisheries Policy that had been agreed only hours before the enlargement negotiations began – a real piece of sharp practice given the importance of fish to Britain and Norway and, as I've already mentioned, a major reason why the Norwegians subsequently voted against entry in their referendum.

All six member states were agreed that, whatever their vintage, none of the elements that went to make up the *acquis* could be re-opened. Negotiations could take place about transition periods, temporary derogations, future policies, potential offsetting agreements, and ways of dealing with what might turn out to be unacceptable situations should they arise. But so far as the *acquis* was concerned, there was, in O'Neill's view, only one option: 'Swallow the lot and swallow it now.'[23] It was the price of arriving late: 'What mattered was to get into the Community, and thereby restore our position at the centre of European affairs which, since 1958, we had lost.'[24]

Within the scope available, O'Neill believed his team did a good job, and they were widely praised at the time. But he accepted that there was an important exception. To clinch a deal on the terms for continued access for New Zealand butter during the transition period, too much was conceded on how the British contribution to the Community budget would rise as it adapted to the 'own resources' system. It was thought that over time other common policies, such as social and regional policies from which Britain stood to gain, would go some way towards compensating for the agricultural imbalance. A vague undertaking was given to the effect that the survival of the Community would require equitable solutions to be found if that didn't happen. Before the decade was out, this issue would come back to poison relations between Britain and its partners as Margaret Thatcher fought to secure a fairer budget settlement.

The detailed negotiations had to succeed to the satisfaction of all the parties involved. But from the outset it was understood by all that, to clinch the deal, the French president, now Georges Pompidou, and the British prime minister would have to reach a personal accord. In practice, as Hurd, now serving as Heath's political secretary, wrote a few years later, Pompidou 'had to believe that Britain was coming into Europe not out of despair, not to make trouble, but as a determined and capable partner'. In Hurd's opinion, 'The winning round of President Pompidou was probably the greatest single feat of Mr Heath's premiership. In these talks he repaired the errors of twenty years of faulty French and British policy.'[25] The rapprochement took place in Paris on 19–20 May 1971, and the joint press conference at which the two leaders announced their agreement was held in the same room at the Élysée Palace in which de Gaulle had pronounced his veto in January 1963. The negotiations were formally wrapped up shortly afterwards.

The final step on the road to fulfilling de Gaulle's prophecy that Heath would lead Britain into the EEC was securing the passage of the necessary legislation through Parliament. It turned out to be the most difficult. As so often happens after a year in office, public opinion had turned against the government. A week after the Élysée press conference, Labour won a by-election at Bromsgrove. The Macclesfield Conservative Association then defiantly chose an anti-EEC candidate, Nick Winterton, for the contest shortly due to take place in that constituency (among the applicants they rejected were future foreign secretary Hurd and the future chancellor of the exchequer Nigel Lawson). In the House of Commons, a group of Conservative anti-marketeers, including Robin Turton, Sir Derek Walker-Smith, and Marten, was working closely with Labour MPs in the Common Market Study Group under Turton's chairpersonship.

In July, the government issued a White Paper on the result of the negotiations, which, though less than frank on the sovereignty issue, indicated that food prices would rise and warned of possible problems ahead over the British budgetary contribution. It also emerged that the Labour Party would oppose entry on the terms brought back by the minister for Europe, Geoffrey Rippon, even though there was no reason to suppose that a Labour negotiator could have done any better. At its autumn party conference, Labour duly decided to do so and to commit itself to re-negotiate the terms, after which the result would be put to the country in a referendum.

After his return from Paris, some of those around the prime minister had urged him to hold an immediate Commons vote on the principle of entry, before opposition to it could gather strength over the summer recess and at the autumn party conferences. The chief whip, Francis Pym, argued against and was proved right. Heath's statement to the House of Commons on 7 July and in a ministerial broadcast a few days later went well, as did a special meeting of the Conservative Central Council. A huge effort was then made to rally support in the constituencies.

On 13 October, the issue was debated at the party conference in Brighton. Powell made an impassioned speech denouncing entry that included the words:

> I do not believe this nation, which has maintained and defended its independence for a thousand years, will now submit to see it merged or lost. Nor did I become a member of our sovereign parliament in order to consent to that sovereignty being abated or transferred. Come what may, I cannot, and I will not.[26]

A significant minority of speakers in the debate supported him, but the delegates gave Heath an overwhelming endorsement by 2,474 votes to 324. The margin of victory undoubtedly overstated the degree of commitment felt by delegates to the government's policy, but it was important as a safeguard for MPs who supported the official line against pressure from members of their constituency associations who opposed it.

During this period, Philip Goodhart, the secretary of the 1922 Committee and MP for Beckenham again raised the question of a referendum. He argued, 'If we are not to be saddled with the charge of dragging the country unwillingly into the Market, then there has to be some visible test of public opinion somewhere at some time.'[27] He was supported by the future Cabinet minister Norman St John Stevas. The proposal failed to gather momentum and was easily quashed by the leadership. Not to be gainsaid, Goodhart went ahead with a referendum in his own constituency, which resulted in a majority for entry.

So, the scene was set for one of the great House of Commons set-piece occasions of the second half of the twentieth century – the six-day debate that began on 21 October on the motion 'That this House approves her Majesty's Government's decision of principle to join the European Communities[28] on the basis of the arrangements which have been negotiated.' Labour imposed a three-line whip against it, but, at the behest of Pym, Heath allowed a free vote on the Conservative side. This turned out to be a master stroke. A Conservative three-line whip would not have brought the party's rebels to heel, while its absence provided those Labour MPs who on principle favoured EEC entry regardless of their colleagues' changes of mind with the cover they needed to vote with their consciences. The result was a far greater victory for the government than had seemed possible when Heath returned from Paris – a majority of 112 with 356 voting for the motion and 244 against. Thirty-nine Conservative anti-marketeers voted with the opposition, but their loss was more than made up for by the sixty-nine Labour rebels who supported the government. The only minister to resign on the issue was Teddy Taylor, from a junior position at the Scottish Office.

I remember the evening well. As we all milled excitedly around in the Aye lobby speculating on what the majority might be while waiting to record our votes with the tellers, I saw Heath standing alone at the back of the crowd. When the voting was finished and the result declared, he retired with a small group of close friends to his flat at the top of Number 10, where he played the First Prelude from Book 1 of Bach's *Well-Tempered Clavier* on his clavichord. One of the friends was Sara Morrison, who recalls that 'Ted did the piano thing instead of conversation at highly stressed or happy moments'.[29]

There were those who thought the celebration might prove premature. The vote, important though it was, had no legal effect. It was an expression of will and opinion. The detailed legislation required to make accession possible had yet to be drafted. The opponents of entry believed there would have to be a long and complex bill that would provide infinite opportunities for delay, disruption, and government defeats. They had reckoned without the new solicitor-general, Sir Geoffrey Howe, who surprised everyone with what he himself later described as a 'coup de théâtre'[30] by producing a bill of only thirty-seven pages with just twelve clauses and four schedules.

The government then set itself the seemingly impossible task of getting it through all its stages in the House of Commons without a single amendment. The first big test was the Second Reading debate from 16 to 19 February 1972. The key question was how many of the rebels on both sides would stick to their guns. When the government's majority dropped to eight, with fifteen Conservatives voting against the government, Powell was exultant. He was so confident that such a narrow margin would be unsustainable over the passage of the bill, as Labour rebels reverted to their normal party loyalty, that he wrote to the French ambassador to warn him that, whatever the government might say, Parliament would prevent Britain from entering the EEC.[31]

There then began what Michael Jopling, who had just joined the Conservative Whips' Office, regards as 'one of the greatest whipping operations of all time'[32] as the bill survived 325 hours of debate, spread over 53 days with 104 divisions, without the government losing a single one. Night after night we tramped through the lobbies regarding ourselves as fortunate if the House rose before midnight. On one occasion, I found myself alone with the prime minister in the Smoking Room between divisions. For want of anything better to say, I asked him how he would like to celebrate victory. 'By staging a programme of operas at each of Europe's great opera houses,' he replied.

The battle over the bill was a war of attrition fought by means of pressure on minorities to follow their party whip regardless of their personal views, but it was conducted without the bitterness and rancour that in later years came to characterise internal Conservative disputes over Europe. There were between thirty and forty irreconcilables, though not all were equally so, and the numbers voting against the different clauses varied. Powell, according to his biographer Simon Heffer, was the only one not to support his party in any one of the 104 divisions.[33] Other opponents of the bill were often willing to give the whips advance warning of their intentions either to vote against the government or to stay away. Relations between the Conservative whips and the Labour rebels were largely in the hands of Tony Royle, a junior Foreign Office minister and former whip. His job was to ensure that enough of them would always be on hand to abstain so as to offset Conservative defectors.

Through the Common Market Study Group (now chaired by Jay), Marten, Walker-Smith, and other Conservative rebels kept in touch with the Labour Party. The rebels' whip was John Biffen, a former enthusiast for entry who had become a member of Powell's inner circle. For their part, Jay and his Labour colleagues were determined to keep a distance between themselves and Powell because of his views on race and immigration.

The arithmetic before each division was sometimes extremely tight, but the government majority never fell below four. Despite the pressures and the ill feeling the battle inevitably provoked, it says much for the tolerance of the Conservative Party at this time that both Marten and Biffen retained their seats on the 1922 Executive throughout.

During the 325 hours of debate, every aspect of EEC membership and what it might mean for Britain was at least touched upon. Powell argued powerfully that the full-hearted consent of the Parliament and people, which Heath had said was required, simply did not exist. He also pointed out that very few Conservative MPs had personally undertaken to support entry in their election addresses. In the light of these considerations, he overcame his distaste for referendums and led nineteen Conservatives into the lobby in a vain attempt to secure one. From the Labour benches, Jay and Benn led calls for a referendum on the grounds that a proposal that involved Parliament surrendering powers should be put to a people's vote.

While the two lead ministers, Rippon and Howe, continued the Macmillan tactic of blurring the potential constitutional implications, Powell and his Conservative allies and, for Labour, Jay, Benn, and Peter Shore spoke eloquently about them. However, they simply failed to gain any traction, and their arguments were dismissed even by some Conservative anti-marketeers. Sir Harry Legge-Bourke (knighted since his previous appearance in these pages) reminded the House that he had opposed the Schuman Plan because of its supranational implications, but said he now thought a close-knit federation less likely to emerge.[34] Angus Maude dismissed the sovereignty argument as being of little importance and based his argument on economic grounds.[35]

As would become apparent during the referendum three years later, sovereignty simply wasn't an issue that stirred most politicians, let alone most people, during the early 1970s. Heath should have taken the opportunity to adopt Kilmuir's advice to be frank with the British people about the implications for sovereignty of joining the EEC. If he had done so, he would have won the argument and the subsequent history of Britain and Europe would have been very different.

Both inside and outside Parliament, the debate was conducted mainly on economic grounds. What principally concerned the protagonists was whether membership of the EEC would help to restore Britain's economic competitiveness, whether British manufacturing industry would benefit, whether the balance of payments would improve, and what would happen to food prices. They were discussed in what now appear to be surprisingly narrow terms. When Heath announced in October, after the bill had passed, that he had agreed to a proposal that the EEC should aim for EMU by 1980, Norman Lamont, elected a few months earlier at a by-election on a pro-entry platform, was horrified. This went way beyond what he thought the EEC was about, but he found 'very little interest among MPs generally about what the proposal might actually mean'.[36] That the idea had been floated by Macmillan to de Gaulle during their discussions in 1962, as will be recalled from Chapter Two, never seems to have been mentioned, if indeed it was generally known about at that time.

When eyes were raised from economic issues and from arguments about the details of the deal, they turned not to constitutional issues, but to Britain's role in the world – whether it would be enhanced by membership and whether it would strengthen the Western Alliance. On this point the protagonists for entry had very much the best of the argument. In 1962 the former American secretary of state Dean Acheson had caused great offence in Britain when he told cadets at the West Point military academy that the problem with Britain was that it 'had lost an empire and had not found a role'.[37] In 1972 many, including me, believed that in joining the EEC the country was taking a decisive step towards resolving that dilemma.

Heath signed the Treaty of Accession at a ceremony in the Palais d'Egmont in Brussels on 22 January 1972. As he entered the building, a young woman threw an ink pot at him and the contents splashed over his head and clothes. To the superstitious this appeared to be a bad omen. And so it transpired – but not immediately.

For a few months, all went well. The European Communities Act became law in October. In the same month, Heath and the prime ministers of Ireland and Denmark joined the leaders of the Six for a summit meeting in Paris, where they all pledged themselves to aim for EMU by 1980 while also agreeing to establish a regional policy. On 1 January 1973 Britain, Ireland, and Denmark formally became members. The Conservative former Cabinet minister and current ambassador in Paris, Sir Christopher Soames, and the man who would have been Labour's minister for Europe, George Thomson, were appointed to be the first British commissioners in Brussels, with the latter given responsibility for regional policy. The Conservative Party also sent a delegation of twelve MPs and six peers to the European Parliament, at that time not directly elected but composed of members of national parliaments. Eight, including their leader, Peter Kirk, were former ministers and two, Walker-Smith and the Ulster Unionist Rafton Pounder, had voted against entry. Labour declined to take up its allocation in the light of its pledge to re-negotiate the entry terms and to hold a referendum.

Disaster struck ten months later with the outbreak of the Yom Kippur War between Israel and several Arab states on 6 October 1973. Oil supplies were seriously disrupted, with Britain and the Netherlands particularly badly hit when the Arabs imposed an embargo on them because of their alleged bias towards Israel. The price of oil on the international markets rose exponentially. By March 1974, when the embargo ended, it had increased by 400 per cent. Everywhere, including in Europe, economic growth came to a grinding halt and inflation ratcheted upwards.

When the EEC was established in the late 1950s, the world was in the middle of the long post-war boom. This enabled the new venture to float off on a rising tide, the best possible context in which to introduce new policies and radical economic changes. In the early 1970s, when Britain joined, the situation was exactly the reverse. Instead of heralding the start of an exciting new era for the EEC, the enlargement coincided with the moment when all new initiatives had to be cut back or postponed. It is impossible to overstate the importance of this difference.

In Britain, the impact of the international crisis was greatly exacerbated by an industrial dispute in the coal industry. At that time, nearly all Britain's electricity was generated by coal, so that when in November the miners' union imposed an overtime ban designed to halve supplies, the effects were calamitous. The government declared a state of emergency and imposed controls on electricity supplies. In the new year, the situation became much worse. Industry and commerce were put on a three-day week and domestic consumers subjected to frequent power cuts while the miners' leaders stepped up their pressure by calling an all-out strike.

To break the deadlock, Heath called a general election for 28 February 1974 on the slogan 'Who governs Britain?' The Conservatives secured a small majority of the popular vote, but Labour became the largest party in the House of Commons with 301 seats to the Conservatives' 297 and the Liberals' 14. The result was so tight that Powell's announcement, three days before polling day, that he had already cast a postal vote for Labour and his urging of others to vote Labour to secure a referendum might well have been the deciding factor.

Wilson returned to power at the head of a minority Labour government. With a re-match regarded as certain, Heath remained as party leader. A second defeat followed in October, after which, in February 1975, he was succeeded by Margaret Thatcher, a story that will be told in Chapter Four.

Heath's tragedy was akin to that of a football captain who, having led his national team through all the qualifying rounds to the World Cup Final, is stretchered off after a few minutes' play. He never had the chance either to develop a British role within the EEC or to guide the country through the process of adjustment to membership. Neither task would have been easy, given the prevailing circumstances and his own inability to express a vision. Whether he would have succeeded we shall never know.

Nor shall we ever know to what extent, if any, he would have taken Kilmuir's advice to be frank with the British people about the full implications of what he was proposing.

In later life, Heath was always very sensitive to accusations that he had not been open about how he wanted the EEC to evolve. In his defence, he drew attention to the clarity with which he had expressed his ambition to achieve EMU. Yet, in his biography, Ziegler recounts an incident in 1973 when the Cabinet minister John Davies submitted a draft to Number 10 of a speech he proposed to make on this subject to the Zurich Economic Society. It contained a passage on how, in the initial stages, the parities of the currencies of the participating countries would have to be irrevocably linked. 'Do we really have to spell this out now?' asked Heath, as he cut it out. 'I am never happy with such pieces. They always do more harm than good.'[38] In the light of this refusal to allow a colleague to make a completely obvious point about monetary union, one has to wonder whether he would ever have been ready to follow Kilmuir's advice.

Following his election defeat, it no longer mattered what Heath might have done. With the new Labour government pledged to re-negotiate the terms of British membership and to put the result to a referendum, all the issues could be debated afresh. The opportunity to secure the people's 'full-hearted consent' had at last arisen. The responsibility for deciding how the Conservative Party should respond to this challenge lay with Thatcher.

4

The 1975 Referendum – Before and After

The emergence of Thatcher as Leader of the Conservative Party in February 1975 was a great deal more surprising than that of Heath ten years earlier. But the two events have three significant similarities. As in 1965, Europe was not an issue in the leadership election. Also, as in 1965, the successful candidate's skilful handling of the Finance Bill in the House of Commons was an important factor in determining the outcome of the leadership election. And finally, just as the election of Heath was to have a profound influence on Britain's role in Europe, so was Thatcher's, though that is a subject for Chapter Five rather than this one.

Although the result of the February 1974 election had been so close, few Conservatives expected to triumph in the inevitable re-match. Heath's government had been discredited, and he had become so unpopular in the party that even his closest associates urged him to stand down from the leadership. He refused, and not just because he still hoped that he might return to Number 10. There was a widespread feeling in some political circles and in the business community that the national crisis was so great that at some point a government of national unity might have to be formed. If that happened, Heath believed he would have an important role to play.

The diary of Cecil King, the former chair of the International Publishing Corporation that published the *Daily Mirror* and

Sunday Pictorial newspapers, conveys something of the flavour of the time. On Sunday 3 March, during the weekend after the election, King thought there would either be a minority Labour government or a coalition between Conservatives, Liberals, and Ian Paisley's Democratic Unionist Party. On 15 June Lord Carrington, his guest at lunch, told him 'there would very possibly be a coalition government', but only 'if things got much worse'. On 16 July Sir Arnold (later Lord) Weinstock, the chief executive of the General Electric Company, told him of a recent conversation with Macmillan in which the former prime minister had said he expected a national government to emerge. On 16 October King records telling Lord Greenhill, the former permanent secretary at the Foreign Office, and Jo Grimond, the former Liberal leader, that he expects 'a dictatorship, either of the right or the left, and much would turn on the attitude of the Army'. Grimond 'thought the political situation had been left to drift too far, and it is now probably too late to do anything to avoid chaos'.[1] All kinds of fevered speculations were circulating during that extraordinary year. During the summer, between the two elections, Ronnie (later Sir Ronald) Grierson, a managing director of the investment bank S. G. Warburg and a vice-chair of General Electric, told me that the only way out of the crisis was a coalition government led by the Duke of Edinburgh.

While these and other similarly wild ideas circulated outside Parliament, Heath hung onto his position, and Conservative MPs were in a ferment about who should succeed him. The delay gave Thatcher the opportunity to emerge from the back of the field.

For most of 1974, the two names frequently mentioned were Willie Whitelaw, as the representative of the One Nation wing of the party, and Sir Keith Joseph, as the champion of the more market-oriented right, with Whitelaw the favourite. The chair of the 1922 committee, Edward Du Cann, and Robert Carr, the shadow chancellor, were other names in the frame. Thatcher was regarded as Joseph's lieutenant rather than as a candidate in her own right. As secretary of state for education in the previous government, she had not been in the first flight of ministers, and the idea of a woman leading a political party still seemed very strange to most people.

Two events catapulted her into contention. The first, on 7 November 1974, was Heath's decision to move her from shadowing the environment portfolio to being Carr's number two on the Treasury team. It looked like a demotion, but turned out to be a golden opportunity. A few days later, the chancellor of the exchequer, Denis Healey, unveiled a budget that included proposals for a Capital Gains Tax and a Capital Transfer Tax. These raised exactly the sort of detailed, complex, and technical issues that played to her forensic strengths. Her performances night after night at the Despatch Box as she picked the measures apart during the bill's committee stage dazzled Labour and Conservative members alike. She completely outshone Carr and even discomfited the formidable Healey. Her reputation soared. Then, on 20 November, Joseph withdrew from the race and, with his support, she took his place as the candidate of the right. A frisson of excitement ran through the party and the country at the hitherto unimaginable prospect of a woman candidate.

Thatcher's good fortune continued into 1975. Airey Neave, a shrewd Parliamentary tactician with a grudge against Heath, offered to take charge of her campaign. For his part, Heath declared that, rather than stand down, he would fight to hold onto his position at the forthcoming leadership election. Whitelaw felt that in that case he could not allow his candidature to proceed unless Heath was knocked out in the first round, in which case he would come in on the second. For his team, of which I was a junior member, this decision was a terrible disappointment.

Heath's decision opened the way for Neave to argue that all those who wanted to stop him should vote for Thatcher on the first ballot to ensure that Heath wouldn't go through to the second. There could then be a straight fight between her and Whitelaw, which, he indicated, he expected Whitelaw to win. The tactic was so successful that a number of those who wanted to vote for Whitelaw in the second round decided not to vote for Heath in the first. I was one of those who abstained. Michael Heseltine was another.[2]

In the first ballot, on 4 February 1975, Thatcher amassed 130 votes against 119 for Heath and 16 for the maverick Hugh Fraser. It was immediately apparent to everyone, including us in the Whitelaw camp, that she had acquired such momentum as to be virtually unstoppable. And so it proved. In the second round, on 11 February, she won 146 votes against 79 for Whitelaw with three other candidates who had decided to enter the fray well behind – Sir Geoffrey Howe and Jim Prior with 19 each and John Peyton with 11.

With what must have been more than a twinge of envy, Barbara Castle, the secretary of state for health and social services, and the most successful woman of her generation in the Labour Party, wrote in her diary, 'The papers are full of Margaret Thatcher, who is looking as radiant as a bride. Who wouldn't after such a successful courtship?'[3] The world looked on in amazement. I remember being asked by an American television interviewer what it would feel like to take orders from a woman.

In the light of subsequent events, this result has often been interpreted as evidence of a clear left–right split in the party. But that was true only up to a point. Many MPs of all persuasions felt that, by challenging Heath, Thatcher had earned the crown and would be a stronger leader than Whitelaw. Among them was Iain MacLeod's biographer Nigel Fisher, an old friend of Whitelaw's, who nonetheless voted for her.[4] A different approach was taken by John Biffen, who supported Thatcher's and Joseph's economic views. As he later recorded in his autobiography, though he kept quiet about it at the time, he voted for Whitelaw on the grounds that he was 'a shrewd fixer' and so more likely to succeed in executing radical economic policies.[5]

The victorious Thatcher wanted, as quickly as possible, to put those splits behind her, to restore party unity, and to shore up her own position. According to her biographer Charles Moore, of the twenty-four colleagues she chose to serve in her Shadow Cabinet only 'perhaps four – Neave, Joseph, Angus Maude and Sally Oppenheim – had voted for her'.[6] In the lower ranks, too, she appointed people known to have voted against her, including me as a junior spokesman on foreign affairs.

No sooner had she taken up her position than she was confronted by the referendum on whether Britain should stay in the EEC on the terms re-negotiated by Wilson. The process had been formally concluded in March and the referendum set for 5 June.

There was no doubt in the minds of those closest to the action that Wilson's aim all along had been to keep Britain in, to reconcile his party to membership, and to put an end to the controversy in the country at large. Bernard Donoughue, the head of the Downing Street Policy Unit, noted in his diary that 'He [Wilson] sees it as a challenge to stay in, get the terms and hold the Labour Party together.'[7] Britain's ambassador to the EEC, Sir Michael Palliser, later told Hugo Young, 'It soon became clear to me that the whole object of the exercise was to keep Britain in, and get something that could be presented to the British as politically adequate.'[8]

What this boiled down to was following Rippon's and O'Neill's precedent of not attempting to unravel the *acquis communautaire* or question the basic tenets of the Treaty of Rome. Wilson also decided not to become too embroiled in the thorny problem of the British budgetary contribution. He thought it was so arcane that no plausible outcome would carry weight with the British electorate, and on that subject settled for what turned out to be a completely useless technical concession. He believed that what would most impress British electors would be to secure better access to the EEC for Australian and New Zealand agricultural products and better terms for produce from the developing countries of the New Commonwealth.

He was successful on both counts. The two groups repaid his efforts in May, the month before the referendum, at a Commonwealth summit at which thirty-two heads of government signed a note supporting British membership of the EEC. In so doing, they provided reassurance to significant bodies of opinion on both the right and the left of the political spectrum, while robbing the No campaigners of an important card. The British budget contribution was left to be dealt with at some future date, by which time, as it turned out, Thatcher would be in charge.

The political class followed the re-negotiation with close interest, the general public much less so. Domestic issues were by far uppermost in the minds of most people. In October 1974 MORI found that only 10 per cent of the electorate regarded Europe as an important issue. Wilson's judgement about how they would react to his terms was, however, correct. When the re-negotiation began, Gallup had recorded a majority of about 5 per cent for pulling out of the EEC. A week after the new terms were announced, it gave those who wanted to stay in a twenty-nine-point lead. From then on, the result of the referendum was never really in doubt.

Wilson's colleagues proved harder to convince. Of the twenty-three members of the Cabinet, seven opposed making a positive recommendation to the electorate. When this question was put in the House of Commons, 145 Labour MPs voted against the motion and 137 in favour with 33 abstentions. More than half of all ministers, counting junior as well as senior, voted against the government. Without the backing of Conservative MPs, Wilson's proposition would not have got through and the referendum could not have been held. Only eight Conservatives opposed it. In normal circumstances, no government could have survived such a result. But, aware of the divisions within his own government and party, Wilson had some time earlier suspended the principle of collective responsibility, so that ministers as well as Labour MPs could vote and campaign on whichever side they wished, both in Parliament and in the country at the forthcoming referendum.

The tone of the Conservative approach was set by Sir Christopher Soames. In a series of seminars for party activists, he argued that entry into the EEC was a Conservative achievement that must be protected from sabotage by the left. Thatcher had no difficulty in subscribing to this line of argument. Europe had never been an issue that excited her. Her approach was utilitarian. She supported British membership because she saw the EEC as a bulwark against communism – a sort of economic complement to NATO – and because it promoted free trade. She argued that the loss of sovereignty involved was largely technical and made clear her opposition to any form of federalism. In the month after she became leader, she told a meeting of students that 'political and economic power in the world today is based much more on continents than oceans – and on populations the size of America, Western Europe, the Soviet bloc and now Japan. Where power resides, there must British influence be exerted.'[9]

The conduct of the campaigns for and against membership was in the hands of two cross-party groups. On the Yes side stood Britain in Europe (BiE), supported by an overwhelming majority of manufacturing and financial companies as well as most of the press and some trade unions. It was flush with funds and could hire whatever expert help it required. Against it stood the National Referendum Campaign (NRC), made up of various anti-Common Market groups plus some trade unions.

By comparison with BiE, it was a very ramshackle affair, short both of money and professional skills. All the weight of the Conservative Party was on the side of BiE, with the party chair, the strongly pro-EEC Peter Thorneycroft, now Lord Thorneycroft, encouraging constituency associations to put their resources at its disposal. Only five Conservative MPs played a significant role in the No campaign – Ronald Bell, Richard Body, Neil Marten, Teddy Taylor, and the former Robin Turton, now Lord Tranmire. Others who provided some help included Biffen, du Cann, Fraser, Walker-Smith, and, from the younger generation, Roger Moate.

Thatcher left no doubt about her support for the Yes campaign and appeared when required at set-piece occasions. The most notable was a Conservative Group for Europe dinner in April at which she appeared alongside Heath and described herself as 'the pupil [who] speaks before the master, because you know more about it than the rest of us'.[10] Another was an eve-of-poll vigil under the statue of Churchill in Parliament Square, presided over by Macmillan. Thatcher allowed herself to be photographed wearing a jersey displaying the flags of all the member states, and she wrote to all Conservative MPs asking them to support the Yes campaign. She did not, however, become actively engaged herself. She left that to Heath and Whitelaw, who worked alongside the Liberal leader, Jeremy Thorpe, under the leadership of Labour's most prominent Europhile, the home secretary, Roy Jenkins.

For Heath, the campaign was a glorious success. Never before had he spoken so effectively and never again would he receive so much acclaim across the political spectrum as he hammered away on the theme of the EEC as a safeguard against another war in Europe. When Castle opposed him in a televised debate at the Oxford Union, she described him as speaking 'with a genuineness which was the most impressive thing I have ever seen from him ... They gave him a standing ovation at the end, and he deserved it for the best example I have ever seen of The Man Who Came Back.'[11] Sadly, this judgement proved premature. The comeback went no further. As soon as the campaign ended, he lapsed into what became known as 'the great sulk', which made him an increasingly lonely figure brooding resentfully against his successor from his seat below the gangway in the House of Commons.

A striking feature of the Yes campaign was the harmony that prevailed among its political heavyweights as they worked together without regard to their party differences. Whitelaw later wrote in his autobiography about how much he had enjoyed working under Jenkins' leadership.[12] Jenkins derived equal pleasure from their association. He also admired the contribution of Heath, his contemporary at Balliol College, Oxford before the war.[13] I can attest from my own experience that what was true of the leaders was equally true of their followers.

Things were different in the No campaign. Its Conservative chair, Neil Marten, and Labour vice-chair, the former Cabinet minister Douglas Jay, had worked together across party lines for many years and got on well together. But its most charismatic Labour orator, Tony Benn, was no team player, refusing ever to share a platform with anybody from another party. So strongly did he feel about this that during a televised debate in a studio modelled on a Commons committee room, he preferred to sit with Labour MPs campaigning for a Yes vote rather than with Conservatives campaigning for a No. His speeches, too, caused problems. Their exaggerated forecasts of the economic disaster that would befall the country if it remained in the EEC drowned out the more considered economic arguments put forward by Jay, Castle, and the secretary of state for trade, Peter Shore. The future foreign secretary Jack Straw, then working for Castle, told her, 'He is losing us the referendum.'[14] Powell was another source of discord. Most of the Labour campaigners wished to keep as far away from him as they could because of his 'rivers of blood' speech and racist reputation, while he was correspondingly cool towards them.

The Yes campaign was fortunate in the timing of the referendum. At most times before, and for many years afterwards, the surpluses generated by the CAP and the issue of food prices would have played into the hands of the No campaign. That was not the case in 1975. Only three years earlier, the Club of Rome, a group of distinguished current and former heads of government, diplomats, scientists, economists, and business leaders, had produced an apocalyptic report entitled *The Limits to Growth* that forecast imminent shortages of food and raw materials. It sold thirty million copies in thirty languages and had an enormous impact on public opinion. The 1974 oil shock and the resulting inflation and disruption to trade patterns appeared to confirm these fears. A sudden shortage of sugar in the summer of 1974 that led Norman Tebbit, then at the outset of his career, to call for rationing, seemed like a harbinger of things to come. In this context, the CAP provided reassurance that Europe would be able to look after itself. As Thatcher wrote in an article for the *Daily Telegraph* on 4 June, the day before the poll, 'I believe that most housewives would rather pay a little more than risk a bare cupboard. In the Common Market we can be sure of something in the larder.'[15]

In other ways, too, membership of the EEC provided reassurance. The three-day week was fresh in people's minds, inflation was running at over 20 per cent, industrial relations remained a serious problem, the IRA was conducting a bombing campaign in mainland Britain, and unemployment had reached levels not seen since the 1930s. The question of whether Britain was any longer governable by conventional means was widely discussed, and not only in political circles. The mood of the country was deeply uncertain and risk averse. When Soames coined the phrase 'this is no time for Britain to be considering leaving a Christmas club, let alone the Common Market', he voiced what many throughout the country felt.[16]

This atmosphere was not conducive to raising alarms about sovereignty or self-government, which were widely regarded as esoteric questions. Polls consistently showed them to be of little concern to voters, whichever way they inclined on the central issue. The Yes campaigners were rarely pressed on the implications of the European Court of Justice for the British legal system, or of the EMU project for the management of the British economy, or what decision-making in Brussels might mean for Parliament. For the most part they were able to frame their argument in terms of protecting jobs, securing food supplies, and the preservation of peace in Europe. To the extent that they were tackled on constitutional issues, they were able to get away with what Hugo Young called 'the golden thread of deceptive reassurance ... nothing you really care about will change'.[17]

The leading No campaigners spoke endlessly about the loss of sovereignty and of national independence, often in exaggerated terms. They alleged that unelected commissioners in Brussels would be able to enact laws and levy taxes and asserted that the EEC was a plot 'to merge Britain with France, Germany, Italy and other countries into a single nation'.[18] In short, in emotional and sometimes misleading language, they raised the issues that Kilmuir had urged Macmillan and Heath to be frank about with the British people in 1961.

They were unable to gain any traction. The electorate was simply not in the mood to listen. Another reason was the character of the individuals who spoke most loudly about these issues. Benn, Powell, the Labour left-winger Michael Foot, and the trade unionist Jack Jones were all regarded as dangerous extremists by the sort of middle-of-the-road voters the No campaign needed to attract. As on economic issues, they drowned out the moderate voices of Marten, Jay, and Shore. An additional problem for the NRC was the nature of some of the organisations that were campaigning separately against the EEC and making much of the independence issue. These included the National Front and other far-right groups, plus the communists on the left. In Ulster, Ian Paisley claimed that a vote to stay in the EEC was a vote for the Pope. Marten did his best to distance the NRC from these unwelcome allies, but he could not entirely prevent them from tarnishing his brand.

Another factor that made life difficult for those warning about threats to sovereignty was the situation within the EEC. The recent establishment of the European Council composed of heads of government as the EEC's supreme body was widely taken to mean that the Commission would be reined in and that the days of supranational ambitions were over. At the same time, the oil shock, which had done such damage to the British economy, had brought further initiatives towards closer integration and, notably, EMU to a halt. The recently elected West German chancellor Helmut Schmidt mocked what he called 'Euro cloud-cuckoo land' and was particularly scathing about EMU, which he described as 'an illusion fostered by idealists who did not understand the problem'.[19] The foreign secretary, Jim Callaghan, who was more of an agnostic about Europe than Wilson, concluded on the basis of his experience attending meetings of the Council of Ministers that, whatever rhetoric ministers from the original Six might use when talking about the future of Europe, there was no need to worry about threats to British sovereignty.

In the light of all this, the great majority of Labour and Conservative supporters of British membership, who did not share Heath's dreams of where it might lead, felt reassured. Just as their predecessors in the 1950s had assumed that the EEC would never get off the ground, so they now believed that it would never fulfil the federalist ambitions inherent in the treaty. It is in this context that 'the golden thread of deceptive reassurance' should be understood.

As 5 June approached, some in the Yes campaign feared a repetition of the referendum in Norway three years earlier when, to the surprise of political leaders and pundits alike, the people had voted against joining the EEC. But no such surprise occurred. When all the votes had been gathered on the following day, it emerged that the margin was 67.2 per cent in favour of staying in the EEC against 32.8 per cent for coming out, on a 64.5 per cent turnout. Every social class and every age group had voted to stay in, as had every region of the United Kingdom, apart from the Shetland Islands and the Western Isles, two small consolation prizes for the Scottish National Party (SNP), which had campaigned strongly against membership.

In the aftermath of the battle, when nobody was very interested in what the losers had to say, the NRC and Marten each issued declarations that turned out to be pregnant with implications for the future. The nation, the NRC said, 'had not committed itself to economic and political union with Europe'. It further warned ministers that they 'should be aware of the consequences of outpacing the consent of the electorate'.[20] In a separate statement, Marten warned that the public had voted for 'the Community as it is' and given no mandate for further integration.[21]

Both Thatcher and Wilson had cause to regard the victorious Yes campaign with some suspicion. At a time when talk of a government of national unity or a coalition was rife, it provided an impressive example of politicians from all three major parties working closely together for a common cause. Jenkins certainly hoped it would lead on to some sort of coming together. At the head of a cross-party campaign and for a few weeks a national leader, he had enjoyed himself enormously. As a first step towards creating something for the future, he 'arranged with Willie Whitelaw that he and I would keep in touch, partly just to reminisce about the great days of the campaign, but partly also to look at political events and to complain about our colleagues'.[22] A couple of dinners were held, but nothing more. Whitelaw had committed himself to Thatcher and, having done so, his loyalty was to her, whatever their differences, just as it had previously been to Heath.

Jenkins was deeply disappointed. In his autobiography, he writes, 'All in all I look back on 1975 as a great missed opportunity for Heath and Whitelaw and a whole regiment of discarded Conservative "wets"[23] as much as for Shirley Williams and Steel and me.'[24] Instead, a few years later in 1981, he, with Shirley Williams, David Owen, and Bill Rogers, broke away from the Labour Party to form the nucleus of the Social Democratic Party. To his further disappointment, they failed to attract any significant Conservative recruits, not even his close friend, Sir Ian Gilmour. Shortly afterwards they joined forces with the Liberals, by then led by David Steel, to form the Liberal Democrats.

Among Conservatives who followed the referendum with special interest were the eighteen MPs and peers who formed the party's delegation to the European Parliament. The outcome enabled them to resume the duties they had taken up there in 1973, and a Labour delegation to join them in Strasbourg, Luxembourg, and Brussels, the three centres in which the Parliament and its committees conducted their business.

The Conservatives had arrived full of enthusiasm and determined to make a constructive contribution to the development of what was at that time a rather toothless body apart from its power, shared with the Council, to approve the Community's annual budget. Until the nominated system was replaced by direct elections in 1979, they were among the Parliament's most active members. Their leader, Peter Kirk, earned widespread respect before his premature death from a heart attack in April 1977. Sir Derek Walker-Smith carved out a new career as chair of the Committee on Legal Affairs. Michael Shaw played a prominent role on the Committee on Budgets. But these were individual contributions. As a group, their impact was limited.

They made three mistakes. The first was to assume that House of Commons procedures and practices could be readily grafted on to a Parliament that had been created on an entirely different model. Aware of the institution's weakness and ineffectiveness, they failed to study the plans for strengthening it that had already been worked out before their arrival and tried to build on British historical precedents, which aroused resentment among other nationalities.

The second was to sit as a group on their own with the addition of three Danish members rather than to join the centre-right Christian Democrat group. This was an understandable decision. They were not after all Christian Democrats. But as the Parliament worked on the basis of consensus building and shifting alliances between three large groups composed of parties from all member states – the Socialists and Liberals were the other two – sitting alone, rather than in the same group as other centre-right parties, inevitably reduced the Conservatives' ability to influence outcomes. And, as things turned out, not only in the European Parliament. Over time the group, renamed the European People's Party (EPP) in 1976, would become a network of cooperation, involving parties within government and without, that would come to exercise a powerful influence within the Council of Ministers and the Commission. In 1992 the Conservatives formed a close association with the EPP, which David Cameron unwisely brought to an end when he became leader of the party many years later.

The third error, as Caroline Jackson argues in her study *The First British MEPs*, was their failure to establish a procedure for

British members of the European Parliament to report back to the British Parliament. As they themselves were members of the House of Commons and the House of Lords, the nominated members felt no need of this. They saw themselves as constituting the necessary link between the two Parliaments. Their leaders, Kirk, and, after his death, Rippon, ensured its effectiveness. The link continued after the introduction of direct elections. Several sitting MPs were elected to be MEPs in 1979, and their leader, Jim Scott-Hopkins, was a former junior minister. But the dual mandate, membership of a national Parliament and the European Parliament, was unsustainable. It involved too much work, too much travel, and too many conflicting commitments. When it was brought to an end with effect from the 1979 European elections, the human link between the House of Commons and the European Parliament went with it. There was then no mechanism or procedure in place to replace it. As Jackson puts it, 'This omission helped to create in Westminster the atmosphere of suspicion of Europe as a threatening territory of the unknown and misunderstood,'[25] an atmosphere that was taking hold in the Conservative Party when she wrote these words in 1993.

The Parliament was not the only European institution to undergo change in the late 1970s. In January 1977, the Commission that had assumed office four years earlier came to an end. Soames and Thomson retired and were replaced by Jenkins, who also became president of the Commission, and me. Callaghan, who had succeeded Wilson as prime minister, had been told by the West German chancellor Schmidt and the French president Giscard d'Estaing that they would support either Jenkins or Heath for the role of Commission president. He had no hesitation in nominating Jenkins, thereby removing a troublesome presence from his own benches and leaving one on Thatcher's.

Ignoring the fact that in 1973 Heath had nominated[26] both British commissioners, the Labour Thomson as well as the

Conservative Soames, Thatcher, as leader of the opposition, thought she would be proposing Soames's successor. The person she had in mind was John Davies, whom she wanted to remove from her Shadow Cabinet. Jenkins disliked the idea of the second British commissioner being a reject and asked Callaghan to approach me. The offer came as a total surprise. I barely knew Jenkins and was quite happy in my role as a junior foreign affairs spokesman. But I had no hesitation in accepting. I regarded the EEC as the most hopeful political experiment to have been undertaken in Europe during the twentieth century and believed it would be greatly to Britain's political and economic benefit to play a leading role in its evolution. The opportunity to be involved at a senior level in these two causes was something I could not turn down, even at the price of offending Thatcher. When I informed her of my decision, she was not pleased. Four years later, however, when our terms of office came to an end in January 1981 and Jenkins retired, she re-nominated me for a second term. I then became the senior British commissioner until January 1985 when I was succeeded by Lord Cockfield.

Like Soames, I saw it as part of my role to maintain close links with the Conservative Party, quite apart from my dealings with the British government. To assist me in that task I reserved one of the five places in my Cabinet, as a commissioner's private office is called, for an individual openly connected to the Conservative Party. This post was initially filled by Dermot Gleeson, who was followed by John Houston and Simon May. All three were outstanding. They acted as a two-way channel of communication with all sections of the party at home and in the European Parliament. They ensured that, besides my official speaking engagements in Britain, I undertook others with Conservative groups up and down the country. They dealt with correspondence from MPs and MEPs, arranged for me to see all those I wanted to see or who wanted to see me, and facilitated visits to

Brussels by groups or individuals from the party headquarters and constituency associations. I also made a point of attending the annual party conference and other party events. In identifying myself with my political party I was in no way unusual. In different ways, most other commissioners did the same. Indeed, my German, Italian, and Irish colleagues only appointed officials to their Cabinets who had links with the political party of which they themselves were members, whereas, apart from Gleeson, Houston, and May, my Cabinet was composed of career civil servants with no known political affiliation.

5

Thatcher's Battles 1979–1991

Just as Heath was responsible for taking Britain into the European Community, so Thatcher was responsible for taking the country out – but in a totally different way. Entry was the result of a determined act of political will on Heath's part. Exit was not the result of any particular action by Thatcher. It was the culmination of a long sequence of events that can be traced back to her attitudes, actions, and statements, and the interpretations that others later put upon them. These culminated in the No vote in the referendum of 2016, but, had things turned out differently at various times along the way, that outcome might have been avoided.

It is not even clear that, had she lived to see it, she would have been pleased with the referendum result. Among Conservative Leavers it is an article of faith that in campaigning for Britain to leave the EU they were acting in accordance with her legacy. But as Charles Powell, for many years her closest adviser on foreign affairs and much else while she was prime minister, and a close friend and adviser until her death in 2013, told me, 'I am convinced that she would never have supported Brexit.'[1] He has written elsewhere:

Margaret Thatcher's aim was to secure Britain's essential interests within the European Community while protecting us from outcomes which would have irretrievably jeopardised

our nationhood, our parliamentary sovereignty and our right
to govern ourselves. She did so in a way that saved us from
having to face the choice between staying and leaving, in her
time at least. Her successors both in Britain and Europe have
been less successful – and are likely to regret it.[2]

Whether she would have welcomed Brexit or not, Thatcher's
relationship with Britain's partners within the EEC was indel-
ibly marked by conflict. During the first part of her premiership,
she carried her Cabinet, MPs, and followers in the country with
her so that many came to regard it as part of the natural order
of things. In the latter period, her approach became a bone of
contention between her and some of her Cabinet colleagues
until, in 1990, her refusal to play a more constructive role in
Europe was among the factors that led to her downfall. As a
result, Euro-scepticism, if not downright hostility to anything so
much as touching on the EU, became identified with her legacy.
From this has flowed many of the problems that made Europe
such a difficult issue for her successors as leaders of the Conservative Party.

When she began, she thought Europe would be a sideshow.
In December 1977, as leader of the opposition, she paid an
official visit to the Commission. She and I talked about what
Britain might try to do in Europe if she won the next election.
As I had been appointed as the commissioner responsible for the
Community budget, we touched on the problem of the British
contribution. She was rigorous and well briefed, but EEC matters
were clearly not among her most pressing concerns. She told me
that when she became prime minister she did not expect to run
her government's European policy. All her time would be taken
up with tackling Britain's economic problems.

In the autumn of 1976, Britain had been forced 'to go cap
in hand', as it was described at the time, to the International

Monetary Fund to ask for the largest single loan that institution had ever made. This had been followed by swingeing budget cuts that had stabilised the economy, but inflation and, above all, industrial relations, remained at crisis levels. At the time of Thatcher's visit to the Commission, many in the EEC were referring to 'the British disease' of 'stagflation', as the combination of high inflation and low growth was called. Worse was to come. The winter of 1978–9 saw so many strikes and so much disruption to normal life that it became known as the 'Winter of Discontent'. In some parts of the country, an unofficial strike by gravediggers meant that the dead could not be buried. In others, refuse went uncollected for weeks while NHS ancillary workers picketed hospital entrances so that only emergency patients could pass through. These events contributed greatly to the Conservative election victory in May 1979. They also made putting the economy to rights by far the government's most important objective, the subject of greatest interest to MPs and party members, and the touchstone by which its success or failure would be judged.

Another major domestic issue was the continuing Troubles in Northern Ireland and the terrorism to which they give rise. The murder of her close friend and mentor Airey Neave in March, just over a month before the election, caused Thatcher herself great personal sorrow. The murders, three months after the election, of Lord Mountbatten while on holiday in the Republic of Ireland and of eighteen British soldiers in Northern Ireland were further examples of the extent of the threat.

Even in the field of external affairs, the EEC was not uppermost in most Conservative minds when Thatcher entered Number 10. The chief priority of MPs and party members alike was to see a settlement of the ongoing crisis in Rhodesia that had begun with its 'illegal' declaration of independence in November 1965. Lord Carrington's success in achieving this when the successor state of Zimbabwe was brought into being and granted legal independence in April 1980 was the Thatcher government's first great triumph. David Howell, then secretary of state for energy, recalls that 'in the press of all these events, European affairs did not impinge greatly on cabinet deliberations'.[3]

It was unfortunate that the Community's budget should have been the first item on Britain's EEC agenda after Thatcher took office. If she and her fellow heads of government, above all President Giscard d'Estaing of France and Chancellor Schmidt of West Germany, had been able to get to know each other and to work together for a while, all might have been different. But that was not possible. The issue, which O'Neill had admitted to not dealing with satisfactorily during the entry negotiations and Wilson had left to fester during his re-negotiation, could no longer be avoided.

As the size of the budget had increased, principally because of more money being spent on the CAP, so had the imbalance in Britain's disfavour, with the result that Britain had become the second-largest contributor after West Germany and, on current trends, would shortly become the largest. As Britain was at that time one of the poorest countries in the EEC, it regarded this situation as being manifestly unfair, and Thatcher was determined to remedy it. In the eyes of the others, it was part of the price of arriving late, and they had no wish to embark on what would amount to a second re-negotiation from which they would be bound to lose out. They also felt that the scale of the problem was generating more political noise than it merited. The Community budget was still tiny by national standards, and the British contribution in 1979 amounted to less than 0.2 per cent of Britain's gross domestic product.[4]

As the former Sir Christopher Soames, now Lord Soames and a member of her government, warned Thatcher, 'the Community had never been renowned for taking decisions without long wrangling'.[5] Even so, had they been wise, Giscard d'Estaing and Schmidt, as the de facto leaders among the heads of government, would, as soon as she arrived among them, have sought to defuse what was clearly an impending crisis. Instead, they made it a test of strength.

This was partly because they misjudged Thatcher's character, which may have owed something to Giscard d'Estaing having remained in touch with Heath after he had lost the Conservative leadership,[6] while Schmidt and Callaghan had always been close. They would also have been well briefed on the political climate in London as she and her chancellor of the exchequer, Sir Geoffrey Howe, grappled with the country's economic problems. Their policies were both unpopular in the country and divisive within the Conservative Party. In that early period of her premiership, there was a widespread belief in political and media circles in London that she might turn out to be a passing aberration, shortly to be replaced by a more conventional Conservative figure.

Throughout this period, the diary of her devoted admirer Alan Clark carries references to the hostility of her 'Heathite' Cabinet colleagues, whom he lists as Lord Carrington, Jim Prior, Sir Ian Gilmour, Michael Heseltine, and Peter Walker, and of how few of the others she could rely on.[7] Although Clark is by no means always a reliable reporter on matters of fact, these entries capture the febrile mood of the time. In September 1981 she was able to strengthen her position with a reshuffle that brought Cecil Parkinson, Nigel Lawson, and Norman Tebbit into the Cabinet. Even so, the Conservatives remained in deep political trouble. The Social Democratic Party, formed by Roy Jenkins after his return from Brussels in January 1981 with the support of David Owen, Shirley Williams, and Bill Rodgers (the so-called Gang of Four), in alliance with the Liberals under David Steel, were carrying all before them and threatening, as the current phrase had it, 'to break the mould of British politics'. Not until Britain's victory in the Falklands War in June 1982 did Thatcher's position in the country as well as the party become unassailable.

After some preliminary skirmishes, the first crunch over the EEC budget came at a meeting of the European Council in November 1979. Only heads of government attended these meetings, and in EEC circles it was thought that an isolated Thatcher would be unable to withstand a combined onslaught from the other leaders. 'This meeting will show what your prime minister is made of,' a senior French official in the Commission said to me with relish as he prepared to set off for Dublin, where the Council was to be held. Confronted with what she considered to be a derisory offer, Thatcher responded by demanding 'my money back', which became her battle cry until the dispute was finally settled. As the argument round the Council table became more heated, Schmidt feigned sleep. When she refused to give in, the French party's cars were drawn up outside with their engines revving in order to emphasise the take-it-or-leave-it nature of what was on offer. Finally, the meeting ended in deadlock.

Writing about the event five years later, the American journalist John Newhouse quoted a Commission official who had been in Dublin as saying that Giscard d'Estaing and Schmidt 'made it clear that she, a mere woman, wouldn't be able to stand up to these two experienced and knowledgeable men in hard negotiation'.[8] In today's climate, it seems incredible that sexism of this sort should have had a part to play in an international negotiation at the highest level. However, I have no doubt that Thatcher's gender was a complicating factor. In May 1980, soon after an interim settlement had been reached that was widely regarded as favourable to the British, Klaus von Dohnanyi, a German minister I knew well, came to see me. 'You must tell your prime minister,' he said, 'that she has hurt my chancellor in his male pride. If things are to be put right between our two countries, she must find a way of making it up to him.' I had to explain that female pride entered into the calculation as well and why I thought it would be unwise to pass on such a message.

I should at this point explain my role in these matters. The Commission was responsible for producing the figures and proposals on the basis of which the member states could negotiate and reach an agreement. As the commissioner responsible for the budget, I and my department were at the centre of the process, although everything the Commission produced had to be agreed, or at least acquiesced in, by all my colleagues. The Commission saw itself as 'the master of the compromise', and its ability to fulfil this function depended on it being trusted by all sides. To achieve that trust, its figures had to be as objective and its proposals as constructive as possible.

With that aim in view, each commissioner was entitled to seek to ensure that the Commission took due account of his (there were no women) country of origin's interests. His overriding duty, however, was not to that country, but to the Commission and its efforts to facilitate an agreement that would be in the interests of the EEC as a whole. This put me in a difficult position. Thatcher believed – and did not hide her feelings – that I should be doing more to help Britain, while members of the European Parliament, sometimes with the connivance of some of my fellow commissioners, accused me of doing too much on Britain's behalf. Jenkins found himself similarly assaulted from both sides. Neither of us found our positions easy.

The budget problem was finally resolved in June 1984, after Jenkins had departed, at a European Council chaired by Giscard d'Estaing's successor, François Mitterrand,[9] at Fontainebleau. Thatcher secured a rebate of 66 per cent on Britain's annual contribution and, of vital importance, binding assurances that the arrangement would last for as long as the problem. This was a better result than anyone would have expected at the time of Dublin. No other European leader – and probably no other British leader – could have held out for so long or secured so much against the opposition of all the rest. But there was a price to pay. Her combative style coupled with her refusal, while the battle was on, to work constructively with other heads of government on other issues left her dangerously isolated. Francis Pym summed up the matter well:

> I would say that Britain's interests cannot be measured by the exact number of pounds in a rebate … the result least in our interests is to have the other nine members of the Community view Britain as a spoilt child who insists on getting her own way at all costs, thus determining them to make life difficult for us in other ways.[10]

When he wrote these words shortly before the agreement was signed, Pym could be accused of grinding an axe, as he had been sacked as foreign secretary a year earlier. But there was wisdom in what he wrote – and not just in terms of Thatcher's relationship with the other leaders and of Britain's with the other member states. The budget row established in the minds of the British people and the British media an image of us against them, of one against the rest, and of Britain constantly battling against the EEC as an alien institution rather than negotiating with the other member states as partners in a common enterprise. This was how Thatcher herself saw it. In her memoirs, she describes, with unconscious folie de grandeur, how the normal outcome of European Councils was 'a British victory on points'[11] without any regard as to whether other countries or the Community as a whole might have benefitted.

For as long as she remained prime minister, she fed this confrontational image. Even in 1982, when, on the outbreak of the crisis that led to the Falklands War, the other member states and the Commission immediately rallied to Britain's support by imposing sanctions on Argentina, she did not modify it. The us-against-them image became fixed in the minds of the British people and the British media and endured until the end of British membership, despite the efforts of John Major and Tony Blair to banish it. The image worked both ways. As Pym warned, it had the effect of making other member states want to get their own back whenever the opportunity arose.

When Thatcher became prime minister in 1979, the Conservative Party had accepted the result of the referendum as a done deal. In the House of Commons, opponents of membership, such as John Biffen, Neil Marten, and Angus Maude, felt able to accept ministerial positions in her government. Other long-standing opponents and doubters (the word 'sceptic' was not yet in use) like Legge-Bourke, Edward du Cann, Hugh Fraser, Richard Body, Teddy Taylor, and Roger Moate were quiescent. They had not resiled from their earlier views. They were ready to be fired up again, if the occasion arose, but for the time being, Europe as an issue was in abeyance. Differences within the government and on the backbenches between those who had faith in how Thatcher and Howe were tackling the country's economic problems and those who doubted them was a far more important and divisive question.

Another factor that kept Conservatives anchored to the pro-Europe cause was what was happening in the Labour Party. Under Michael Foot's leadership from November 1980 to October 1983, the party had reverted to opposing EEC membership. For as long as Labour espoused an anti-EEC position, the Conservative Party had a powerful incentive to remain the 'Party of Europe', as it had sometimes referred to itself during the 1970s.

Outside Westminster, the party's support for Europe was far from total. Survey evidence gathered by Anthony Forster[12] shows that in 1979, 42 per cent of Conservative voters still supported withdrawal as against 46 percent who opposed it. The latter group were, with very few exceptions, not idealists thinking in terms of a united Europe. They supported membership because they looked to the EEC to deliver tangible economic benefits to Britain and would judge it on that basis. This squares with my recollection of the reception I received and the questions that were put to me when I spoke at Conservative gatherings up and down the country.

The most notable champion of the European cause was Heath. This weakened rather than strengthened its appeal to most MPs and their constituents, as he combined that position with a public display of disdain for the person and policies of his successor. For MPs and others in the party, too close an identification with Europe and too much enthusiasm for it ran the risk of appearing to be an expression of disloyalty to Thatcher. This had important long-term consequences, as it meant that constituency associations became disinclined to choose Parliamentary candidates who were enthusiastic about Europe, and preferred those who took a more combative approach in line with the prime minister's. Their attitude to Europe was never the only criterion against which would-be Parliamentary candidates were judged. Some constituency associations cared more about the issue than others, but as the 1980s progressed and Thatcher's rows with other EEC member states intensified, so, with each succeeding general election, the new intake of MPs became more hard line.

In the circumstances of 1979, Thatcher's approach to Europe was perfectly attuned to the mix of attitudes and emotions on the issue swirling around within the Conservative Party. It united those who had campaigned on the Yes and No sides in the referendum, on a platform that combined support for British membership of the EEC with a robust defence of British interests. Over time the resolution of the budget dispute came to be seen in Conservative circles, and to be presented to the country, as one of the government's battle honours alongside the victories over the Argentinians in the Falklands War and over the miners when, led by Arthur Scargill, they again tried to bring the country to a halt in their great strike of 1984–5.

This triumphalism blinded those who rejoiced in it to the fact that for many on the continent, the EEC had a deeper purpose than simply the removal of barriers to trade and the creation of various common policies. The European Council that brought together the heads of government and the Council of Ministers in its various formations – foreign affairs, finance, agriculture, etc – were at times fields of combat on which national interests were ruthlessly pursued. Nonetheless, the Community was also widely perceived in other member states to be an instrument, in the words of the Treaty of Rome, for achieving 'an ever closer union among the peoples of Europe'. To ignore this dimension was to make the same mistake that Conservative leaders, and others in Britain, had made in the 1950s when they believed that the EEC would never get off the ground.

Britain did not have to interpret this aspiration in the same way as its partners. The word 'union' could be interpreted in different ways, and it wasn't necessary to accept the more extreme. From the very beginning, even before Britain arrived on the scene, there had been a tension between Monnet's dream of a supranational or federal model and de Gaulle's of a *Europe des patries*. Many in the other member states subscribed to the latter. But it was necessary to respect the Monnet dream, to take account of the influence it had on policy formation in other member states and, which was not at all the same thing, the extent to which it was exploited to camouflage the pursuit of national interests. This was something Thatcher could not do. She just could not understand how some of her fellow heads of government regarded the EEC, how it fitted into their countries' historical experience, and the hopes they had invested in it. She remarks at one point in her autobiography on 'the quintessentially un-English outlook displayed by the Community'.[13] She is referring to her difficulties over the budget, but this reflection encapsulates how she felt towards the whole enterprise.

In these circumstances, a major clash over how the EEC should develop was sooner or later almost inevitable. In the immediate aftermath of Fontainebleau, however, there was a general mood of optimism and a determination to move the EEC forward after the bitterness and sterility of the budget dispute. It was agreed on all sides that the next big project should be the creation of a single market for goods and services within the EEC by removing all the barriers to trade, visible and invisible, that still existed to protect domestic producers and special interests. This fulfilled one of the central objectives of the Treaty of Rome. It was also very much in line both with what had attracted Conservatives, including Thatcher, to the EEC in the first place, and with her government's attack on vested interests and restrictive practices within the British domestic market.

With her approval, the heads of government appointed the French socialist and former finance minister Jacques Delors as president of the Commission from January 1985 to tackle the task. To assist him she sent her Cabinet colleague Lord Cockfield to replace me as the senior British commissioner,[14] and he was duly given the Internal Markets and Services portfolio. In a long career he had been at different times a civil servant, a businessman, and most recently a government minister, a combination that ideally qualified him to produce a blueprint for the single market. I was pleased to be returning home after eight years in Brussels, yet sad to be leaving just as Britain was about to play a leading and constructive role in Community affairs. Howe, who had become foreign secretary in June 1983, captured the mood of the moment when he later wrote, '1985 was the year in which we were able, now that the budget problem was out of the way to make a powerfully distinctive contribution to the "relaunch" of the Community.'[15]

Delors and Cockfield drew up a plan for the establishment of a single market by 31 December 1992. At the same time, work was going on to create a new framework within which the member states could coordinate their foreign policies, another project of which Thatcher approved. The two streams came together in what was called the Single European Act (SEA). After being endorsed by the heads of government, it was brought before the House of Commons in April 1986.

The significance of this measure can hardly be overstated. It was the first major revision of the Treaty of Rome since 1957. It also represented a massive extension of 'Community compe- tence', or supranational control, since it required many of the decisions needed to complete the single market programme to be made by qualified majority voting[16] rather than by unanim- ity. Normally this would have been anathema to Thatcher. But as a practical woman she recognised that it was only by these means that the Delors programme could be completed. So, just as de Gaulle, in the early 1960s, had swallowed his objections to the surrender of national sovereignty involved in qualified majority voting on the CAP because he believed that policy to be in the French interest, so did Thatcher in the 1980s on the single market, because she believed it to be in the British interest. In both cases, the leaders put pragmatism before principle because they felt this best served their national interest.

Her mastery of the Conservative Party was such that, despite the surrender of sovereignty that it involved, the European Com- munities (Amendment) Bill, the means by which the SEA was to be incorporated into British law, was driven through all its stages in the House of Commons in six days: a total contrast with the fifty-three days that had been required to pass the original European Communities Act in 1972. It will be recalled that among the most consistent opponents of the 1972 act had been John Biffen. Now, as leader of the House in the Thatcher government, it fell to him to propose the guillotine motion that drastically limited the time allowed for debate on the details of the new bill. He later described this action as 'the only major blot of apostasy on my Eurosceptic record'. That Bill Cash, one of the most consistent of all upholders of British sovereignty, was 'with me in the lobby'[17] provided some consolation. Very few MPs were prepared to stand out against the prime minister. Among those who did by refusing to vote for the bill on Second Reading were Jonathan Aitken, Nick Budgen, Edward du Cann, Harvey Proctor, and Teddy Taylor.

Once the bill was through, Europe faded into the background as an issue within the Conservative Party. It didn't merit a mention in the speeches Thatcher delivered at either the 1986 or the 1987 party conferences. Nor did it feature much in the 1987 general election. At the meeting held beforehand to brief all Parliamentary candidates, Norman Fowler, then secretary of state for health and social services, noticed that Europe didn't give rise to a single question. But this did not mean that the issue was dead. In his words, 'it was a smouldering fire'.[18]

Sooner or later, that fire was bound to flare up. The British government regarded the single market programme as an end in itself. Others took the view that it should form part, an important part but still only a part, of a broader suite of measures. Across the continent a majority of governments and political parties thought that on its own a single market could not command widespread popular support. They wanted it to be matched by a social dimension covering such issues as working conditions, hours of work, equal opportunities, notice periods, and consultation between management and labour. It was also widely, though not universally, believed that a single market should be matched by a single currency at the heart of EMU, the goal to which the original Six plus Britain, Ireland, and Denmark had pledged themselves in 1972. A committee chaired by Delors on which Britain was represented was set up to work towards this goal. Thatcher was strongly, indeed viscerally, opposed to both ideas.

In 1989 the fall of the Berlin Wall added a further complication to the Community's agenda, in the form of German unification. Thatcher could have welcomed that historic event as the victorious outcome of the Cold War in which she had been such a steadfast warrior, and therefore as something to celebrate. Her dislike and distrust of the Germans[19] prevented her from doing so, and the unification of their country made her still more unhappy with the way the EEC was developing. Any one of these issues had the potential to cause ructions between Britain and its partners. Together they formed a toxic mix.

The social dimension was the first to give trouble when, in July 1988, Delors set out to the European Parliament his vision of what it should comprise. He hoped, he said, to bring it to fruition by 1995, which would mean that '80 per cent of our economic legislation, perhaps even fiscal and social as well' would need to be taken by 'the beginnings of a European government'.[20] To Thatcher, this was nothing less than a power grab by the Commission. To some extent it was, but Delors was not speaking simply for himself or the Commission. His vision, if not its details, enjoyed widespread support in the national legislatures of most of the political parties represented in the Parliament.

Worse was to come. On 7 September, Delors took the battle literally onto Thatcher's own ground by addressing the annual conference of the Trades Union Congress (TUC) at Brighton. In an eloquent speech in which he sought the support of the British Labour movement for his ideas, he talked of how workers' rights could be safeguarded and collective bargaining conducted at the

European rather than the national level. After the numerous defeats the unions had suffered at the hands of the Thatcher government since 1979, this was music to the ears of the assembled delegates, who gave him a standing ovation. In the longer term, the speech paved the way for the Labour Party to slough off its anti-Europeanism and, in 1997, to return to power under Blair, committed to active British membership.

The price Delors paid for this success was the alienation of Thatcher and the Conservative Party. Nothing could have done more than this speech to inflame her or to anger Conservative supporters. Over the previous nine years, the British economy had become one of the most successful in Europe. It was widely believed, and not only by Conservative voters, that among the reasons for this had been the government's success in taming the trade unions and improving industrial relations. By holding out to the unions the prospect of winning back at the European level the power and influence they had lost at the national level, Delors was appealing over the prime minister's head to an important and hostile section of her own electorate. Such a challenge could not go unanswered. It was bound to call forth a strong riposte.

The riposte came in a speech Thatcher gave to the College of Europe in Bruges on 20 September. Now one of the most famous that she ever delivered, it is remembered as being almost a declaration of independence from the EEC. The reality was far more nuanced. The engagement had been in her diary for some time, and the Foreign Office had seen it as an opportunity for the prime minister to set out her vision for the future of Europe. With its emphasis on 'willing and active cooperation between independent sovereign states' and on opening the EEC's doors to the countries of Eastern Europe once they had thrown off their communist shackles, the speech does so in ringing terms. And it makes clear Britain's continued commitment to the Community enterprise: 'Britain does not dream of some cosy, isolated existence on the fringes of the European Community. Our destiny is in Europe, as part of the Community.'[21]

But it is not for this passage that the speech is remembered. Its most famous and enduring passage is: 'We have not successfully rolled back the frontiers of the state in Britain, only to see them re-imposed at a European level, with a European super-state exercising a new dominance from Brussels.'[22] Another that resonated widely in the Conservative Party and beyond was that 'working more closely does not require power to be centralised in Brussels or decisions to be taken by an appointed bureaucracy'.[23] This was not an accurate representation of the reality. She knew very well that while the Commission proposed policies and executed them, the key decision-makers were the ministers from national governments meeting in the Council of Ministers. But that is a quibble. The significance of these two passages was that they linked Thatcher's opposition to Delors' ambitions, and the ambitions of those who wanted to create EMU, with her domestic themes of opposition to socialism and an overmighty state.

She returned to the Bruges themes in her speech to the Conservative Party's 1988 annual conference in Brighton in October. 'Ours is the true European ideal,' she stated at one point. At another, 'No one should doubt Britain's whole-hearted commitment to Europe.' She again linked her attacks on Delors' ambitions with her hostility to socialism and the overmighty state: 'We haven't worked all these years to free Britain from the paralysis of socialism to see it creep in through the back door of central control and bureaucracy from Brussels.'[24]

Brighton was more than a repetition of Bruges. The second speech contained important passages that explained the nature and limitations of Thatcher's belief in Europe. In one, she set out 'the choice between two kinds of Europe – a Europe based on the widest possible freedom of enterprise – or a Europe governed by socialist methods of centralised control'. In another, she said, 'There is no doubt what the Community's founders intended. The Treaty of Rome is a charter of economic liberty which they knew was the essential condition for personal and political liberty.'[25] This was a highly idiosyncratic interpretation of the treaty. She made no mention of the aspiration of 'ever closer union', which others believed Europe-wide social and monetary policies would help to bring about. The speech set the boundaries beyond which she would not be prepared to go. In Brussels, discussions, in which British representatives were participating, were already well advanced on both social policy and EMU, including the establishment of a European Central Bank and a common currency. Further clashes were therefore inevitable.

Speeches become historic landmarks not just because of their contents, but because of the impact they have at the time they were delivered and thereafter. That is certainly the case with Bruges. Its impact was both immediate and enduring. In EEC capitals, it was seen as a frontal assault on the Community's institutions and above all the Commission. Hitherto, other leaders had believed, or wished to believe, that their differences with Thatcher were about matters of degree rather than principle. After Bruges, that was not possible. They had to accept that, whatever might be the position of some ministers in her government, she was opposed on principle to the direction in which they wished to travel.

The pity of it is that she chose to present her case in such confrontational terms. That wasn't necessary to make her point. In theory, the EEC worked on the principle that all member states should proceed at the same pace towards the same destination. In practice, ideas were already circulating for how they might proceed at different rates, with some states not participating in some projects. I speculated on these possibilities, variously known in the jargon as 'two-speed' or 'multi-speed', as 'concentric circles' or 'variable geometry', in the book I published in 1986, a year after my return from Brussels.[26] Others were doing so elsewhere in the Community. If Thatcher had drawn her line around what she could and could not accept in this context, the reactions would have been quite different.

Howe was dismayed and saw Bruges and its aftermath as the moment at which Thatcher escaped from 'the collective responsibility of the Heath cabinet' and 'the European policies she had accepted as a member of that same government'.[27] This was not true. Her own speeches had always made clear that her concept of the EEC and the nature of British involvement in it was more limited than Heath's.

In Michael Heseltine's opinion, 'She had divided the Tory Party and unleashed the hounds that were to eat away at the vitals of the party from then on.'[28] This also was not true. She had exposed divisions rather than creating them. Within the government, one of the most important of those divisions related to the EEC's Exchange Rate Mechanism (ERM). Under this arrangement, the exchange rates of the various EEC currencies were linked in bands that limited the extent to which they could fluctuate against each other. It was seen by the participants as a preliminary to the creation of a common currency. Both the chancellor of the exchequer, Nigel Lawson, and the foreign secretary, Sir Geoffrey Howe, wished Britain to put sterling into the ERM, though for different reasons. Lawson saw it as a means of reducing the rate of inflation by in effect linking sterling to the Deutsche Mark and free riding on Germany's strict monetary policy. He did not want Britain to join EMU. Howe, on the other hand, was open, but not committed, to going the whole hog. Only much later, after the Euro had been successfully introduced, did he become fully convinced that Britain should join EMU.[29]

Heseltine had been outside the government since resigning as secretary of state for defence in January 1986 over the Westland affair: a dispute with the prime minister over whether the helicopter company of that name should be rescued in conjunction with a European or an American company. He had since established himself as a 'king over the water' rival-in-waiting to Thatcher. As her attitude to Europe had hardened, he had become increasingly identified with closer engagement with the EEC, besides offering alternative approaches in other policy areas.

Among MPs, the divisions were about both economic and European policy. Those broadly speaking on the left tended to be in favour of Heseltine's approach to the EEC and to be unhappy with the extent to which Thatcher was pushing her free market agenda in domestic politics. Those on the right took the opposite view on both points and were thrilled by Bruges. The speech brought together their two priorities: on the one hand, resistance to how the EEC was developing, and on the other, support for the Thatcher government's domestic achievements and continuing domestic agenda. The speech therefore acted as a sort of flag around which they could gather, and as a symbol of their support for the prime minister against those they saw as seeking to undermine her position. The speech attracted support outside Parliament, too, and led a group of businessmen with close links to Thatcher to fund a Friends of Bruges Group to promote an agenda based on its underlying philosophy. Under the chairpersonship of Lord Harris of High Cross, who had previously built up the Institute of Economic Affairs into the most influential free-market think tank in the country, it quickly became a force to be reckoned with.

To complicate matters, Thatcher's personal position when she travelled to Bruges was far less strong than it had been when she drove the European Communities (Amendment) Act through the House of Commons. A rise in inflation and interest rates was part of the problem. Discontent within the party and the country over her increasingly hectoring and domineering style after nearly ten years in power was another. By far the biggest was the poll tax, a measure with which she herself was closely identified. Officially called the Community Charge and passed into law less than two months before the Bruges speech was delivered, it was a new form of local taxation to replace the rates that, since time immemorial, had provided the means by which local authorities raised revenues to pay for their services. Its central feature, a flat-rate per-capita tax on every adult, at a rate set by the local authority, created public outrage and led to the largest mass demonstrations the country had seen since Suez and would see until the protests against the second Iraq War.

The government's difficulties were compounded by the elections to the European Parliament in June 1989. Thatcher would have liked them to provide a popular endorsement of the Bruges approach to the EEC, and the party ran an overtly anti-Brussels campaign. Its slogan as polling day approached was the rather absurd 'If you don't vote Conservative next Thursday, you'll live on a diet of Brussels.' Whatever appeal this might have had if the election had been fought on European issues, it fell totally flat in the face of concerns about the state of the economy and the poll tax that dominated the electoral battle. The result was a Conservative rout. The party lost twelve of its forty-five seats, and its 34 per cent share of the vote was its lowest in any election since the introduction of universal suffrage in 1928. For the first time, Labour became the largest British party in the European Parliament, and for the first time since 1979 it could realistically hope that it might be in sight of victory at the next general election.

Thereafter, nothing went right for Thatcher. In the EEC she found herself on the losing side in two interrelated battles. In one, she failed to block progress towards EMU and the European Central Bank that would lie at its heart. In the other, after the fall of the Berlin Wall in November 1989, she failed to delay progress towards the rapid unification of East and West Germany. President Mitterrand had been just as unhappy as she was at the prospect of a united Germany. Unlike her, he accepted the inevitable while demanding a price for his support in the form of closer integration within the EEC to constrain the growth of German power. He saw EMU as a means of achieving this.[30] To Thatcher, such a solution was a case of the cure being as bad as the disease, and her disillusionment with the EEC increased still further.

At home, the poll tax continued to undermine the government's popularity and her own personal authority, as MPs began to fear for their political futures at the next election. Both ministers and backbenchers were also becoming increasingly restive about the extent to which she was combining a domineering style towards them with reliance on her unelected advisers. The two most frequently mentioned were Charles Powell, her foreign affairs adviser, and Bernard Ingham, her chief press officer. But it was the role of Alan Walters, her economic adviser, that brought matters to a head when, on 26 October 1989, Lawson resigned over what he regarded as Walters' undue influence. His resignation sent shock waves through the party. The shrewd and experienced Norman Fowler, who had served in the Cabinet since 1979, wrote in his diary, 'My first thoughts tonight are that this really must be the beginning of the end of the Thatcher years.'[31]

Shortly afterwards, the hitherto unknown backbencher Sir Anthony Meyer put himself forward as a pro-Europe stalking horse candidate to challenge Thatcher for the leadership. He hoped this would flush out Heseltine or some other more prominent figure to take over the role. Nobody came forward, and he went head-to-head with her himself. When the result was announced on 5 December, it was not Thatcher's 314 votes that attracted attention, but Meyer's 33 and the 27 abstentions. That sixty MPs should have failed to support the prime minister was a serious blow to her prestige, and it might have been much worse. After it was over, Tristan Garel-Jones, a party whip famous for his mastery of the dark arts of whipping, told the new chancellor of the exchequer, John Major, that 'apart from the sixty malcontents, a further hundred members of the parliamentary party had needed to be "worked on" to keep them onside'.[32] The implications were clear. Meyer had paved the way for a more serious challenge, unless the prime minister could restore the government's popularity and win back the support of the disillusioned.[33]

The extent of her problem was underlined three months later, in March 1990, when the Conservatives lost the safe seat of Mid Staffordshire to Labour on a swing of some 20 per cent. It peaked with a dramatic sequence of events the following October. The month began quietly with Thatcher finally conceding to Major what she had always denied Lawson, by agreeing that sterling should enter the ERM, which took place on the 5th. Then came the shock of the Eastbourne by-election on the 18th, when this traditionally rock-solid Conservative seat was lost to the Liberal Democrats on another 20 per cent swing.[34] It ended in the House of Commons when, while reporting on a recent European Council, Thatcher allowed all her pent frustrations with the EEC to burst forth. After listing what she described as Delors' ambitions for the European Parliament, the Commission, and the Council of Ministers, she cried 'No! No! No!' to each, while the anti-Europeans on the Conservative benches cheered her on.

For Howe, the way she presented the issues and the spin put on her words by Ingham were the last straw. In the previous June, he had almost resigned when Thatcher moved him from the Foreign Office to become leader of the House of Commons; she had since treated him with a disdain their Cabinet colleagues were embarrassed to witness.[35] Now he hesitated no longer and resigned on 1 November.

Howe had never throughout his long career been regarded as a great orator. Denis Healey had famously compared being attacked by him with being mauled by a dead sheep. His resignation speech, however, turned out to be the most devastating in living memory. The passage in which, with a cricketing analogy, he accused the prime minister of undermining her own government's European policy was particularly telling, as it illustrated both how difficult she had become to work with and the point of difference between them. It meant, too, that Heseltine could no longer credibly remain in the wings and forced him to put his case to the test by challenging her for the leadership.

Thatcher's approach to Europe has thus come to be seen as creating the crisis that led to her downfall. It certainly played a major part, but it was the occasion rather than the underlying cause. The fundamental problem was the government's unpopularity as a result of the poll tax and the deteriorating economic situation, which in turn had led to the by-election defeats that made MPs and ministers fear for their own electoral lives. Europe was not a problem with the electorate at that time. Indeed, as Peter Kellner, the former chair of the YouGov polling organisation, has pointed out, membership of the EEC was never more popular with the British public than in November 1990, with 56 per cent regarding membership of the EEC as a good thing and only 13 per cent as bad.[36]

Yet it is the part played by Europe in Thatcher's downfall that has lived on in the party's collective memory as an iconic moment in an endless battle for the party's soul. This is because, once the poll tax had been replaced by the council tax with effect from the 1993–4 financial year, the public quickly lost interest in local taxation. The Europe issue, by contrast, became increasingly contentious as the EEC moved down the track towards EMU and brought forward other initiatives.

As the implications for national sovereignty in the way in

which Europe was moving became increasingly apparent, it was inevitable that there would be differences of opinion within the Conservative Party and among the public at large over what Britain's role in the enterprise should be. As recounted in Chapter Two, Kilmuir had warned Macmillan and Heath that, unless the implications for British sovereignty were faced up to and argued out at the time of Britain's entry into the EEC, they would cause trouble in the future. That future had now arrived, and the consequential trouble was further compounded by the bitterness generated by the fall of Thatcher.

This was not inevitable. Had her campaign against Heseltine been better managed, she might have survived, albeit badly wounded, to go later in a manner that did not involve Europe. Major and the new foreign secretary, Douglas Hurd, proposed and seconded her candidature to continue in office. The Cabinet lined up to support her, and she was widely expected to win. Heseltine was regarded by many MPs and ministers as a divisive figure whose style would exacerbate divisions rather than unite the party. Another factor was a feeling among some MPs – and only MPs had the right to vote on the leadership – that, after all her past achievements, she should not be forced out in this manner. They knew, too, that she remained popular among the members of their constituency associations. As it was, however, she had a completely inadequate campaign manager in Peter Morrison, who took too much for granted and failed to mobilise supporters or work on doubters with the energy and skill the task required.

When the votes were counted on 20 November, the margin of failure was desperately close. Thatcher won 204 votes to Heseltine's 152, a clear majority but four short of the absolute majority plus 15 per cent laid down in the rules. She was to have no second chance. In sometimes highly emotional one-to-one meetings, her Cabinet colleagues warned her that, having failed

to win on the first ballot, she had lost the confidence of the party.
If she went on, they warned, she would get fewer votes in the
second round. She took their advice and stepped down.

At that point, Major and Hurd, whom I supported, came
forward to resist the Heseltine challenge, and it emerged that
Heseltine too had shot his bolt. In a second round of voting on
27 November, Major came top with 185 votes to Heseltine's 131
and Hurd's 56. This time Major was two short of the target, but
Heseltine and Hurd immediately withdrew and he was declared
the winner. He owed his victory in large measure to the support
of Thatcher loyalists who, at her behest, voted for him partly to
defeat Heseltine, and partly in the mistaken belief that his views
were close to hers and that he would look to her for guidance.
When, during his premiership, she and they discovered their
mistake, they would exact their revenge. Hurd, one of the most
consistent pro-Europeans since his days with Heath, and a moderate on economic policy, had a better understanding of where
Major stood on the political spectrum. Two days before the poll,
he told Max Hastings, the editor of the *Daily Telegraph*, which
was supporting his own bid, that he thought 'John Major would
be a very good Prime Minister'.[37]

From today's perspective, with Old Etonian Boris Johnson
having followed closely on the heels of his Eton contemporary
David Cameron, one of the oddest features of the 1990 leadership contest is the extent to which being an Old Etonian told
against Hurd. Never again, it was argued, at least by those who
opposed him, could the Conservative Party be led by someone
with the privileged background that Eton represented.

6

Things Fall Apart 1991–1997

The fall of Margaret Thatcher was the most dramatic event anyone active in politics at that time had ever witnessed. In her prime, she had totally dominated the government, her party, and political debate. Even as her authority ebbed, she was often able to impose her will and remained dangerous to cross. It had become almost impossible to imagine Number 10 without her. When the Cabinet gathered for the first time under his premiership, John Major looked round at his colleagues and captured their mood with the words 'Who would have thought it?'[1]

Who, indeed? Although he had held two of the great offices of state, Major had been in the House of Commons for only eleven years. By comparison with his immediate predecessors when they became prime minister, his experience at the highest levels of government was very slight, as was his public profile. Those of his colleagues who had worked closely with him rated him highly and knew where he stood on the political spectrum, as Douglas Hurd's judgement quoted in Chapter Five shows. Most of the Parliamentary party, however, knew little about him. Thatcher's influence, exercised on his behalf because he wasn't Heseltine and because she thought he would be the continuity candidate, had propelled him into Number 10. Once he was through the door, it became a handicap as he set out to become his own man, as he was bound to do.

Major's inheritance was a difficult one. In the Middle East,

British troops, as part of an American-led force, were poised to go to war with Saddam Hussein's Iraq to liberate Kuwait. At home, the government was deeply unpopular because of the poll tax and the economy, which was going into recession, with inflation again rising ominously. After such a long period of Conservative rule, the backbenches were awash with MPs whose ambitions had in one way or another been disappointed and who were no longer susceptible to pressure from the whips.

And there was the split in the party over Europe. 'I was standing,' Major writes in his autobiography, 'astride a deep and widening fissure in the party.'[2] It will be recalled from Chapter Two that in 1961, when he launched his abortive bid to take Britain into the EEC, Macmillan had feared that he would break the Conservative Party as Peel had done in 1846 over the repeal of the Corn Laws. Major had the same fear: 'Sir Robert Peel was forever at my side: in all my time in Downing Street he was never to leave it.'[3]

The ghost of Peel was matched by the presence of Thatcher. No other prime minister has been so consistently undermined by their immediate predecessor as Major was by her. She was driven by resentment, just as Heath had been when she took over from him. Norman Fowler[4] served in Cabinet under the leadership of both. In his view, 'Both were bitter about the manner of their departure; neither was ready to leave the public stage; both felt that policy on Europe was of fundamental importance.'[5] But there the similarity ended. Heath had lost three elections while Thatcher had won three. When Heath lost power, he was unpopular among party members and a lonely figure in the House of Commons. He had few supporters, and he retreated into what became known as 'the great sulk'. Thatcher, by contrast, had many supporters in the House of Commons and was still extremely popular among party members, many of whom were outraged by her fall.

They were inclined to take it out on those MPs who had voted against her. One was David Nicholson, who thought his vote had been secret, but whose name was then included on a list of their supporters put out by the Heseltine camp. The news provoked suggestions in his Taunton constituency association that he should be de-selected, which, fortunately for him, fell away as its members rallied round to defend council seats in a difficult upcoming local election.[6]

Disregarding the contribution that the poll tax and economic problems had made to her downfall, Thatcher felt she had been ousted by pro-Europe politicians over a disagreement about European policy. This would remain her version of events until the end of her life. She was determined to fight back and was encouraged by her admirers to do so – and not just about Europe. With their support, she would defend her legacy whenever it appeared to be threatened. She was infuriated by the return of Heseltine to the government as environment secretary and, as the months passed, she found the extent to which Major was deviating from what she thought she would have done increasingly distressing.

Among the MPs most attached to her was the diarist, former junior minister, and Eurosceptic Michael Spicer. His entries during the first months of 1991 provide a running commentary on meetings with a shifting cast of characters, including Norman Tebbit, Nicholas Ridley, Bill Cash, and George Gardiner among others, to form a Thatcher support group on the backbenches with links to sympathetic members of the Cabinet. They saw their role as guiding Thatcher as well as supporting her. Ridley in fact described them as the 'Steering Wheel Group'. In April, when she wanted to attack plans being brought forward by Heseltine to replace the poll tax, Spicer records, 'We remind her that Europe is the big issue.'[7]

Meanwhile, the government was enjoying a successful

induction. Abroad, the Gulf War with Iraq was brought to a successful conclusion. At home, the government's image with the general public was transformed by the change from a familiar and dominant figure at the top to a new one with an unthreatening and consensual style of leadership. The sense that there had been a real change was enhanced by several high-profile actions. The poll tax was replaced by a new council tax at much lower rates, and the previously frozen child benefits were uprated. The government also brought an end to a long-running NHS scandal by providing proper compensation for haemophiliacs who had been given HIV-infected blood. In another highly symbolic gesture, at a time when gay people had not yet achieved equality before the law, Major held a well-publicised meeting with the gay actor and activist Ian McKellen at Number 10.

In the EEC, Major set about mending fences with his fellow leaders, above all Chancellor Kohl of Germany, both because of his importance and because Thatcher had been on particularly bad terms with him. In the course of this courtship, he made a speech in Bonn[8] that created almost as much stir as the one Thatcher had given at Bruges. It contained these words that Major himself had drafted: 'My aim for Britain in the Community can be simply stated. I want us to be where we belong. At the heart of Europe. Working with our partners in building the future.'[9] Nothing could have sounded more different from those passages in the Bruges speech that everyone remembered. But, like Bruges, there was far more to the speech than the headlines. Much of its substance could have been expressed by Thatcher when she was prime minister, though the tone was certainly different from hers and her views were no longer the same as those she had held when she was in office. Both in the EEC and in Britain, the speech was understood to herald a change in the government's approach to Europe.

The test would come at the European Council due to be held

at Maastricht in the Netherlands at the end of the year. Important decisions were scheduled to be taken there on a timetable for the introduction of a single currency and on the establishment of the social policy that had aroused Thatcher's ire when Delors spoke about it in 1988 at the European Parliament and the TUC. Caught, as he was, between the Scylla of what his fellow heads of government wanted to achieve and the Charybdis of what his party, and indeed his country, were willing to accept, Major appeared to be in an impossible position.

Signs of the trouble awaiting him if he failed to navigate a way past these two mythical sea monsters were clearly visible. In November, standing as the pro-government candidate, Fowler, who had retired from being a minister, challenged the arch-Eurosceptic Cash for the chairpersonship of the Conservative backbench European Committee. In what turned out to be a trial of strength, he won, but Cash, backed by Tebbit, racked up ninety votes.

Shortly afterwards, in a Commons debate on the government's negotiating mandate for the Maastricht conference, Thatcher put down her marker, and a very important one it turned to be. Reversing her previously well-known opposition to referendums, she demanded that the government give a commitment to hold a referendum before any decision to take Britain into a single currency. At the time, the significance of this proposal lay in the fact that, in the run up to an international negotiation, a former prime minister was advocating a position different from that of her successor, who believed that the matter should be decided by Parliament. Its long-term significance was far greater. It staked out what would become a key European battleground over the next twenty-five years, both within the Conservative Party and beyond. What began as a debate about holding a referendum before joining the single currency spread to holding one on other European issues and finally, in 2016, culminated in the referendum on whether Britain should remain in or leave the EU. Having dropped her bombshell, Thatcher then voted in favour of the negotiating position the government had put to the House. Tebbit plus five of her other supporters abstained.

The greatest misgivings are sometimes followed by the greatest successes: so it was for Major in Maastricht. The conference, along with his subsequent victory in the 1992 general election, turned out to be one of the two great triumphs of his premiership and was hailed as such at the time. After the election, it was overshadowed by the difficulties the government had in getting the consequential legislation through the House of Commons, to the point where the word 'Maastricht' became a synonym for Parliamentary hell. But that does nothing to detract from the initial success.

Major flew out to Maastricht on 8 December 1991. He was accompanied, as was usual on these occasions, by the foreign secretary, still Douglas Hurd, and the new chancellor of the exchequer, Norman Lamont. Because of the sensitivity and political importance of the items on the agenda, he also took Tristan Garel-Jones (who had left the Whips' Office to become minister of state for Europe, reporting to Hurd), to maintain close and continuous contact with the mood of the party at home, something Thatcher had never felt the need to do. Garel-Jones's personality and experience ideally qualified him to act as a two-way communicator, allowing Major at any given moment to weigh up the balance of the pressures he was under from colleagues in London on the one hand, and European leaders round the negotiating table on the other.

The key to Major's success at Maastricht lay in safeguarding what he regarded as vital British interests while not trying to prevent others from pursuing theirs. In practice, this meant that he did not stand in the way of the EEC's commitment to establish a common currency, in return for which he secured Britain's permanent right not to be a part of it. If, at some point in the future, Britain might wish to opt in to the currency, it retained the right to do so, but for as long as it wished it could stay out. The commitment of the other member states to a social policy was dealt with in a similarly ingenious fashion. To take account of British objections and to avoid a British veto, the other members set up a new Social Chapter outside the conventional Treaty-of-Rome-based EEC framework. In due course, under Blair's Labour government, Britain chose to opt in to the social policy. It remained outside the single currency to the end.

These were not the only matters agreed at Maastricht. Another that fitted well with British ideas on how Europe should be organised, while running counter to the federalist theory of how Europe should evolve, was that law and order, foreign affairs, and defence should be dealt with on an inter-state basis, as distinct from within the conventional Community framework. On the other side of the ledger, the conference agreed that once the treaty establishing the new arrangements came into force, what had, up till then, been known as the EEC would become the European Union (EU). This was not a matter of mere words. The EU would become an entity in interna-tional law and those who lived within its borders would become citizens of the EU as well as of their own countries. Significant as they were, these two agreements received less attention in Britain at the time.

Never again would Major enjoy such widespread praise as on his return from Maastricht. *The Times* called the negotiation 'an emphatic success for John Major and his new European diplo-macy'. The *Daily Mail* led its front page with 'Major wins by a knock-out'. *The Sun* described how 'Major played the winning hand in Europe'. The *Daily Telegraph*'s Brussels correspondent, Boris Johnson, was equally lavish in his praise. 'In almost every sense, it was a copybook triumph for Mr Major, the stuff of

Foreign Office dreams,' he wrote. The paper's leader was head-
lined 'Out of the summit and into the light'.[10]

When he entered the House of Commons on 11 December to
make the customary prime ministerial statement on what had
transpired at the Council, Major was greeted with cheers and
the waving of order papers. Spicer, rather sourly, described the
scene as 'triumphalist'.[11] Major himself later wrote, 'It was the
modern equivalent of a Roman triumph.'[12] Thatcher sat silently
on the backbenches but, on the following night, when Major
attended a party to celebrate her fortieth wedding anniversary,
she was quoted as saying, 'I'm absolutely thrilled – I do con-
gratulate him.'[13]

At this point the government had to decide whether to carry
the legislation required to implement the Maastricht agreements
through Parliament before the forthcoming general election,
which could not be delayed beyond June 1992, or to leave it to
be dealt with by whichever party won the election. There was no
danger of the ratification going astray. Labour, influenced in no
small measure by Delors' 1988 speech to the TUC, was by this
time back in the pro-EEC camp and would take up the baton if
it was returned to power. Nor was there any need to hurry, since
other member states, especially those with constitutions requiring a referendum, would take many months to complete their
processes.

If the legislation had been brought forward before the election,
it would have passed with much less difficulty than turned out
to be the case after the election. But ministers could not foresee
the future and decided against this course of action. There were
other bills they wanted to get through before the dissolution,
and the business managers didn't want to subject MPs to a
crowded Parliamentary timetable when they would be wanting
to spend more time in their constituencies. Major and his closest
colleagues were also sensitive to the continuing divisions within

the party over Europe and had no wish to see them put on public display in a pre-election period.

Many pro-Europeans, including me, believed that the Maastricht deal had gone a long way towards resolving Britain's underlying EEC problems. Taken together, the establishment of the opt-out principle and the flexibility shown over how to handle law and order, foreign affairs, and defence had, we felt, demonstrated an impressive willingness by the Community to adapt to changing circumstances. The foundations had been laid, we thought, for a more flexible Community in which Britain would feel more comfortable than in the past. In our view, the agreement brought back by Major provided Britain with the opportunity to enjoy the benefits of EU membership without being forced down the federalist road against its will. This in turn, we thought, would enable it to break out of the confrontational mindset established by Thatcher.

Others remained unconvinced. They thought the flexibility would prove to be a chimera and that Britain would find itself dragged down a slippery slope by powerful forces it could not resist towards the sort of federal structure they abhorred.

The rise of Germany loomed large in the minds of this latter group, two of whom helped to set the Eurosceptic agenda even before the Maastricht conference took place. In July 1990, while Thatcher was still in office, her close ally Nicholas Ridley, in an interview with Dominic Lawson of *The Spectator*, described EMU as 'all a German racket designed to take over the whole of Europe' and equated handing over sovereignty to the Commission, in itself a ludicrous misrepresentation, with giving it to Hitler.[14] The executive of the 1922 Committee told Thatcher that if Ridley remained in the government, his views would be taken to be hers, which her biographer Charles Moore says 'to a large extent they were', and, with great reluctance, she felt she had to ask him to resign.[15] Bill Cash harked back further in a book he published in 1991 that warned against the dangers of a federal Europe under German domination. He pointed out that 'It was forty years from the foundation of the German Empire to the outbreak of the First Word War,' and concluded that 'Plans for a united Europe stray into the darkest political territory'.[16]

The imminence of a general election meant that neither side, unless provoked, wanted to argue these matters out on the floor of the House of Commons or in the country. The then party chair, Chris Patten,[17] has told me:

> Our gut feeling was that this was a dog that had not barked, and we did not see any point in waking it up before the election campaign. Our general sentiment was that Europe was not going to be much of a problem before or during the campaign and this turned out to be true.[18]

Nobody seems to have taken a contrary view, and when the election took place in April it looked as if the decision had been proved right.

During the campaign, Labour, under the leadership of Neil Kinnock, looked to be on their way back to power after thirteen years of opposition. For most of the campaign, the pollsters were predicting this, and it was what most people expected. With the economy still in the doldrums, it seemed inconceivable that the Conservatives could win an unprecedented fourth consecutive election victory. But, as in 1970, the Conservatives with a widely underrated leader came from behind to win when the polls opened on 9 April. As the Labour MP, Giles Radice,[19] recorded in his diary, 'The big swing to Labour that most of the commentators and the polls predicted has simply not materialised.'[20] The Conservative majority was greatly reduced from 102 to 21, but that was as nothing compared with the fact of the victory. Moreover, although the party's majority was well down, its share of the total vote was only 0.3 per cent less than when Thatcher won her landslide in 1987. For Major, the victory was an astounding personal triumph.

The extent to which Thatcher begrudged him his laurels may be judged from an article she wrote two weeks later for the American magazine *Newsweek*, in which she declared, 'I don't accept the idea that all of a sudden Major is his own man. He has been prime minister for seventeen months and he has inherited all these great achievements of the past eleven and a half years ... There isn't such a thing as Majorism,' she added, whereas 'Thatcherism will live. It will live long after Thatcher has died.'[21] She was to be proved right in her boast, and justifiably so; her achievements were considerable. What she failed to appreciate when she wrote that article, and later, was her debt to Major for securing them. If a pre-Blair Labour Party had won the 1992 election, it would have reversed much of what she had done. By winning the 1992 election, Major ensured that there could be no going back. She never gave him the credit he deserved for that.

In terms of Europe, the centre of gravity among the Conservative MPs who returned to Westminster after the election was quite different from where it had been in the previous Parliament. The fifty or so members of the old House who had retired had been overwhelmingly pro-Europe, whereas a majority of their younger successors took a more sceptical view, among them the future Conservative Party leader Iain Duncan Smith. As I have previously explained, constituency associations throughout the 1980s, feeling it was what Thatcher wanted, had tended to select Parliamentary candidates with a sceptical approach to Europe, a trend that reached an apotheosis with the 1992 intake. Many of these new members had grown up in politics looking to her for inspiration, to such a degree that when they reached the House of Commons they were sometimes referred to as 'Thatcher's children'. There was another factor at play as well. Labour's formerly anti-EEC stance had helped to anchor the Conservative Party to the pro-Europe cause. In 1992, not only was Labour in favour of British membership, it wanted to sign up to the Social Chapter, a position that made it seem more pro-Europe than the Conservatives and was bound to push Conservatives in the opposite direction.

The Maastricht bill – officially another European Communities (Amendment) Bill – received its second reading on 21 May 1992. In an effort to smoke out Conservative rebels, Labour abstained. Their tactic succeeded to the extent that twenty-two Conservatives joined those Labour MPs still opposed to the EEC in voting against; not enough, however, to worry the whips unduly. The bill passed by 336 votes to 92. With the committee stage set to begin on 4 June, it looked as if the measure would complete its Parliamentary passage in good time to leave the autumn free for the government to get on with fulfilling its manifesto commitments.

Then came a thunderbolt from out of the blue. On 2 June, against all expectations, the Danes rejected the Maastricht Treaty in a referendum by 50.7 to 49.3 per cent. Never before or since has a vote in another country had a more direct impact on British politics. If even one EEC country failed to ratify the treaty, it would be null and void. It thus immediately became apparent to MPs of all persuasions that what they had assumed to be the treaty's inevitable progression towards ratification by all the member states could no longer be taken for granted. The rebels saw their opportunity and swung into action. The following morning, Spicer, with his colleagues James Cran and Christopher Gill, tabled a motion calling for a 'fresh start with the future development of the EEC' and 'proceeded to scour the House of Commons to sign up other supporters. Within a few hours ninety-one Conservative backbenchers had signed'.[22]

The government faced a dilemma. They knew that the Danish

referendum was not the end of the story. Further negotiations would be held to meet the Danish objections and save the treaty. In fact, as Britain would be holding the six-month rotating presidency of the European Council from 1 July till the end of the year, it would be Major's responsibility to lead the search for a compromise. Even if he was successful in finding one, another possibility still had to be taken into account. The French, too, were committed to holding a referendum, scheduled for 20 September, and reports from Paris suggested that the outcome was too close to call.

Against this uncertain background, ministers had to decide whether to stick with their original timetable or to pause the process until the Danish and French situations had clarified. Opinion was divided. Major records that the European whip, David Davis, was for pressing on. So was Garel-Jones. The chief whip, Richard Ryder,[23] believed the bill could be passed, but only at the price of 'blood all over the floor'.[24] Eventually the whips advised Major to delay, and he agreed.

On the information available to him at the time, this appeared to be the right decision. On the one hand, to go ahead was certain to cause divisions within the party; on the other, there was the uncertainty across the Channel. If no agreement could be reached with the Danes, or if the French should vote No, there would no longer be any need for the bill. Ministers hoped desperately for a French No, but in what became known as the '*petit oui*', they voted Yes by 50.8 percent to 49.2. As a result, with work still in progress on squaring the Danes, the bill had to be brought back to the Commons. Fate decreed that it would do so in the worst possible circumstances: after the national humiliation of Black Wednesday.

That fateful day was Wednesday 16 September 1992, when sterling fell out of the European ERM. At this distance of time, and from the perspective of a world in which we have become accustomed to freely floating exchange rates, this event sounds somewhat esoteric. But in 1992 the government had staked its reputation on preventing it and spent many billions of pounds from the nation's reserves in failing to do so. When it happened, it was widely regarded as being the economic equivalent of the 1956 Suez debacle. As the chancellor who had put sterling into the ERM, Major's reputation was severely damaged when it fell out, as was that of the current chancellor, Norman Lamont – rather unfairly, as he had not been an advocate of membership in the first place. Everyone also remembered that Thatcher had never liked the idea.

It will be recalled that Lawson and Major had wanted to put sterling into the ERM to reduce the rate of inflation. In that respect, their judgement was vindicated. Before sterling's entry, inflation was running at 10 per cent and rising. When it was forced out, the rate was 3.7 per cent and falling. Whether inflation could have been brought under control as effectively by other means will never be known. The fact that it was substantially reduced during the period of sterling's membership of the ERM contributed to Britain's economic recovery after 1992.

The underlying cause of the crisis had nothing to do with Britain. It stemmed from the unification of Germany in 1990. By midsummer 1992, the German government's programme for financing that historic enterprise was turning out to be inflationary and to require the raising of German interest rates. This in turn was pushing up the value of the Deutsche Mark on world currency markets and putting downward pressure on the other ERM currencies linked to it. The pound, the French franc, and the Italian lira were all feeling this pressure. Britain was caught between a rock and a hard place. With its own economy in the early stages of coming out of a recession, the last thing it needed was higher interest rates. But these would have to be introduced to maintain the value of sterling against the Deutsche Mark to the extent required to remain within the ERM.

As summer turned into autumn, the currency markets increasingly took the view that sterling would have to be devalued, while Major and Lamont tried to persuade the Germans to lower their interest rates. At the same time, worries in the currency markets about the French franc because of what might happen in the French referendum were further increasing the upward pressure on the Deutsche Mark.

When the lira was devalued with the agreement of the other ERM member states while remaining within the system, the Germans made a small interest rate cut. Instead of helping to stabilise the pound, this move convinced the markets that the pound would be the next currency to fall. At this point, or indeed earlier, the British could have similarly sought to agree a devaluation with their partners that would have kept the pound within the system. Instead, they threw their reserves into an almighty battle to defend their currency's existing value, and ratcheted up interest rates. The final attempt to lift the siege came on Black Wednesday with the announcement that the Bank of England's Minimum Lending Rate would rise to 15 per cent. As it became clear that, even at this level, sterling would not be able to hold its value against the Deutsche Mark and remain within the ERM, Lamont rescinded the interest rate increase and announced the suspension of Britain's membership of the ERM.

The course of the battle, the failure of the Germans to provide help when it was needed, which they subsequently did to the French, and the final defeat at the hands of the currency speculators seared the minds of all who had been closely involved, officials and politicians alike. From that moment on, the odds would always be against Britain locking itself into the single currency. George Soros, the most high-profile of the speculators, became internationally famous as the man 'who broke the Bank of England', and Lamont's young research assistant, David Cameron, drew his own conclusions.

The impact of the ERM defeat on the government's standing was immense. Its reputation for competence was dealt a blow from which it never recovered. Support for British membership of the EU was similarly damaged. Yet, paradoxically, the debacle turned out to be good for the economy. The combination of the reduction in the rate of inflation during the ERM period with the devaluation of sterling when it left the mechanism provided the foundation on which first Lamont and then, from May 1993 onwards, his successor, Ken Clarke,[25] were able to build an impressive economic recovery based on a policy of targeting inflation.

At the time, however, all that mattered politically was the debacle and the fact that it was associated with Europe. When the party members gathered in Brighton in early October for their annual conference, Fowler, who had become chair after the general election, recorded events in his diary:

> Any criticism of things European is greeted with cheers and thunderous applause from a section of the audience ... When Tebbit is called they erupt with joy ... There then follows five minutes in which he knifes John Major ... The very nastiest display I have ever seen by a senior Conservative politician.[26]

These divisions played into the hands of the Labour Party. Labour was in favour of the Maastricht Treaty, but objected to aspects of the government's bill, notably the opt-out from the Social Chapter. It also opposed the government's domestic agenda, of which a highly controversial pit closure programme was a prominent feature. It was, therefore, prepared to cooperate with those Conservatives who opposed the bill in the hope of bringing the government down or, at the least, keeping it so bogged down with this measure that it would be unable to make progress on anything else. The most committed pro-Europeans on the Labour benches were unhappy with the tactic, but it had the support of the majority, which meant that the bill could only be passed after a long and hazardous period of Parliamentary trench warfare. A key role was played by George Robertson, the opposition spokesman on Europe and future secretary-general of NATO,[27] in proposing amendments that secured the support of Conservative rebels while keeping pro-Europe Labour MPs on board.

Just how hazardous the bill's passage would be became apparent when ministers decided to hold a 'paving' debate before getting down to the committee stage, in the hope that this would ease the bill's passage. As the day of the debate approached, it looked as if the government might even be defeated, thereby throwing the prime minister himself into jeopardy. On the day itself, Major records, 'Norman Tebbit [recently ennobled] made regular trips from the House of Lords to lurk in the Members' lobby outside the Whips' Office urging dissent.'[28] Until the very end the outcome was uncertain, with the government finally winning one of the divisions by only three votes, thanks to the support of the Liberals. Twenty-six Conservatives defied the strongest of three-line whips to vote against the government, while six others abstained.

Contrasting views of the result that cast light on the feelings of the participants are provided by the Spicer and Radice diaries. On the evening of the vote, Spicer wrote, 'Had everyone voted the way they said they would I would not have ended up with a few colleagues in Theresa Gorman's house at 11 pm miserably wondering why we lost by three votes.'[29] In his entry for the following day, Radice recorded, 'I feel absolutely shattered. I have not only lost my voice but feel personally diminished by having to vote the way I did.'[30]

A crisis was thereby avoided, but at a price. Many Conservative MPs worried about what would happen if the Danes were to say No in the second referendum they had agreed to hold after reaching a new agreement with the other member states. As he approached the division lobby, Major saw a backbencher called Michael Carttiss hesitating about what to do. When Major requested his support, Carttiss asked what would happen should the Danes again vote No. Major responded by promising that, to guard against that eventuality, the bill would not be completed until the Danes had decided.[31] As they were not planning to hold their referendum until May 1993, this meant a further prolongation of the government's agony until the summer, and a whole winter to get through before then.

On the surface, the passage of the bill through its committee and report stages resembled that of the original European Communities Bill in 1972 – the same constant uncertainty about how votes would go, Conservative rebels with their own whips colluding with Labour, and some Herculean feats of Parliamentary endurance. Cash personally crafted 240 amendments to the bill and defied three-line whips forty-seven times. But there were two important differences. One was that in 1972 the debate was simply about the bill: there were no extraneous influences. In 1992–3, EEC business continued, and new issues were constantly arising that added fuel to the domestic debate. The other difference was that in 1972, as the rebel John Biffen recorded, relations within the party remained cordial. In 1992–3, they were so embittered that, at a very late stage in the long drawn-out battle, the government could only get its business through by submitting itself to a vote of confidence.

After the original bill was passed, those who had opposed British entry maintained their position, but normal life and party discipline resumed. After the Maastricht bill finally reached the statute book in July 1993, this did not happen. The bitterness continued to contaminate every aspect of life within the Parliamentary party and to infect attitudes and decisions on issues which had nothing to do with Europe. Major himself inadvertently contributed to the ill feeling on the day after the bill was passed when, through a microphone he thought was turned off, he was heard to describe his opponents as 'bastards'. Exactly whom he was referring to wasn't clear, but that hardly mattered. The word was enough. The rebels adopted it as a badge of honour, with one of their number, Theresa Gorman, making it the title of a book she wrote on how they had tried to stop the Maastricht bill.[32]

The next serious Europe-related crisis blew up in November 1994 over a bill to implement an increase in the EU's financial 'own resources'. Faced once again with opposition from Conservative rebels, ministers decided to wield the big stick by making the bill's passage an issue of confidence in the government itself, which meant that the whip would be withdrawn from any Conservative MP who failed to support it. Instead of confirming the leadership's authority over the backbenchers, the tactic badly misfired when eight of them abstained: Teddy Taylor, Theresa Gorman, Richard Shepherd, Christopher Gill, John Wilkinson, Tony Marlow, Nicholas Budgen, and Michael Carttiss. The veteran Sir Richard Body (knighted in 1986) then announced that, as he was with them in spirit, he would resign the whip in protest at their expulsion and join them. No such breakdown in party discipline had been seen before, but far from losing out as a result of their punishment, the 'Whipless Nine' received more attention than ever from the media and party activists. A few months later, they were able to return to the fold under a face-saving formula that enabled them to claim victory.

By the summer of 1995, it had become clear that things could no longer go on as they were. With the precedent of the challenges to Thatcher's leadership still fresh in people's minds, speculation was rife in Parliament and the media that there would be a coup against Major. Rather than allow his opponents to take the initiative, he launched a pre-emptive strike by resigning the leadership of the party and submitting himself to re-election. The Welsh secretary, John Redwood, then resigned from the Cabinet to raise the Eurosceptic and Thatcherite standard against him. Few MPs could take Redwood seriously as a potential prime minister. The question was not so much whether he would win as whether he would damage Major sufficiently to force him to resign. Waiting in the wings and ostentatiously preparing to come in on a second round was the far more formidable Michael Portillo, the secretary of state for employment, who was widely regarded as the ablest proponent of Eurosceptic and right-wing economic views. Thatcher herself was known to regard him as a worthy successor to her mantle.

Major's task was harder than that of Heath and Thatcher when they had been challenged and had failed to achieve victory in the first round. Like them, he had to secure a majority of the Parliamentary party plus a margin of 15 per cent, which on this occasion meant 165 votes. But both he and everyone else understood that in practice he had to do significantly better than that to secure enough credibility to be sure of surviving until 1997, when the next general election would have to be held. With the Conservative-supporting newspapers vociferously against him, this was a tall order, and it was not at all clear what they and MPs would regard as adequate. He privately set himself a target of 215 and would have resigned had he secured anything less. In the event, he won 218. His campaign team instantly went before the television and radio interviewers to claim a decisive victory, and it was accepted as such.

Major reshuffled his government and continued in office until being routed at the polls in 1997. Before that, the government was to become embroiled in one more incident to complete the sequence of things falling apart over Europe during his premiership. This was the so-called BSE crisis that began in March 1996, when the Cabinet was made aware that there might be a link between bovine spongiform encephalopathy, a disease known for some years to be present in Britain's beef herd, and a new strain of a human brain disease known as Creutzfeldt-Jakob disease (CJD). The announcement of the possible link provoked immediate alarm in this country and, after a short delay, led to a decision by the EU Standing Veterinary Committee to impose a temporary ban on all British beef exports. The committee took this action not because it believed the link had been established, but because, for as long as any doubt existed, such a ban was necessary to protect the domestic sales and exports of beef producers in other EU member states.

The committee's decision infuriated British ministers, who regarded the ban as disproportionate and an incitement to panic both in Britain and elsewhere. Their response was to embark on a campaign to obstruct all decision-making in the EU that required a unanimous decision, a reaction that in turn was regarded as totally unreasonable in other member states. The standoff did not last long. By the end of June, an agreement was reached that linked the lifting of the ban to a slaughter programme in Britain. It enabled normal EU business to be resumed, although the slaughter programme and the final removal of the ban took much longer. The damage done to the idea of Britain as part of a great European cooperative enterprise was incalculable. The sense that membership of the EU involved Britain in constant battles with the other member states was confirmed. The idea that Maastricht had created the conditions that would allow Britain to live more comfortably in the EU than before was dead.

The Eurosceptic wing of the party continued to gain strength, with its focus on opposing British entry into the single currency, to prevent which it was demanding that a referendum should be held, as suggested by Thatcher in 1991. There was in fact no immediate likelihood of the government taking any such step. It had neither the desire nor the strength to do so, but it did not wish to close off long-term options. Its policy was not to rule out the possibility of joining while not committing itself to doing so, a position supported by many of those, including me, who were most committed to supporting active British engagement in the EU, whatever our views on the single currency as such. Eventually, in 1996, Major promised that if, after the next election, a Conservative government was returned to power and wished to join the single currency, it would put the matter to a referendum. The Leader of the Labour Party, Tony Blair, felt obliged to follow suit.

By then, the idea that a referendum should be held before any future changes in the European treaties had acquired a talismanic status among the Eurosceptics. There was also a powerful new voice arguing the case, in the form of the Anglo-French millionaire Sir James Goldsmith, who, in November 1994, had set up his Referendum Party with the wider aim of achieving a referendum on the nature of Britain's membership of the EU. He was on friendly terms with Thatcher, whose close friend, Sir Alastair McAlpine, a former Conservative Party treasurer, and Carla Powell, the wife of Charles, were among his most enthusiastic supporters. He himself, besides running his own party, provided financial support to the European Foundation, a body run by Bill Cash to which Thatcher herself made at least one contribution of £5,000.[33] Together Goldsmith and Cash, with Thatcher's blessing, constituted the cutting edge of Euroscepticism on the centre-right of British politics, and would continue to do so for some time to come.

They were not, however, its most radical element. A month before the establishment of Goldsmith's party, an important taboo had been broken by the former chancellor Norman Lamont when he became the first senior Conservative politician to raise the idea that Britain should contemplate the possibility of leaving the EU. His private conversations as chancellor with his fellow finance ministers about how they saw the future of Europe and what they thought their children's attitude to it would be had made him aware of how different their hopes and ideas were from his own.[34] The forecast of his French opposite number, Pierre Bérégovoy, when they were together at a meeting in New York, that 'we were inevitably going to see a United States of Europe' had made a particular impression on him. He had shared his thoughts since leaving the government in May 1993 with others at meetings of a Conservative Philosophy Group hosted by his fellow MP, Jonathan Aitken.[35] In October 1994 he aired them for the first time at a fringe meeting of the party conference in Bournemouth.

He did so in guarded terms, stopping well short of actually advocating withdrawal, but three phrases in his speech stood out. In one, he said, 'It has recently been said that the option of leaving the Community is unthinkable. I believe this attitude is simplistic.' In another, 'As a former Chancellor I can only say that I cannot pinpoint a single concrete advantage that unambiguously comes to this country because of our membership of the European Union.' In a third, 'I do not suggest that Britain should today unilaterally withdraw from Europe. But the issue may well return to the political agenda.' Guarded though they were, these words were enough for his speech to lead *The Times* on the following morning[36] and to generate widespread debate thereafter. It was the moment the Leave genie was let out of the bottle, although some years would elapse before that option would be openly espoused by a significant number of Conservative MPs.

Worries about the implications of becoming involved with moves towards some kind of EU had existed within the Conservative Party since the 1950s. They were among the reasons why the governments of Churchill and Eden had declined to become involved with the creation of the ECSC and the EEC.

Heath overcame them when he took the country into the EEC in 1973. The party's contribution to the Yes victory in the 1975 referendum confirmed that decision. They were revived in 1988 by Delors' speeches to the TUC and the European Parliament about how far he saw European integration being carried, and they were articulated by Thatcher's response to Delors in her Bruges speech. They gained further strength from the circumstances in which she lost the premiership.

The ERM debacle and the divisions over the Maastricht bill took the process of alienation from the EU an important step further. They combined to embed a strand of active hostility to continued British membership within the Conservative psyche, as distinct from the doubts and discomfort that had always been there. The constitutional historian Vernon Bogdanor makes a telling point when he refers in this context to pro-European Conservatives being 'delegitimised' within the party and a 'commitment' to Europe coming to be seen as an 'aberration, a departure from true Conservatism'.[37]

This attitude was, over time, greatly reinforced by the newspapers that generally support the Conservative Party. In 1992 Paul Dacre became editor of the *Daily Mail* and turned it into a strident voice of Euroscepticism. Rupert Murdoch, with *The Times*, the *Sunday Times*, and *The Sun* under his control, had been close to Thatcher and always deeply sceptical of the EEC and all its works. So, too, had Conrad Black,[38] who controlled the Telegraph Media Group, including *The Spectator*, from 1986 to 2004, since when it has maintained the same line under different ownership.

Through their editorials and the way they have framed news stories, these papers have over the years fed their readers an unrelenting diet of Euroscepticism. An early and highly effective exponent of this genre was Boris Johnson in his role as the *Daily Telegraph*'s Brussels correspondent from 1989 to 1994.

They have also given more space to commentators and columnists of a Eurosceptic bent than to pro-Europeans. Politicians in search of support have naturally taken note of this bias. Another more subtle influence has been at work as well. The personal and social links between politicians and those who write about politics have always been very close. The two groups interact with each other in all kinds of ways. From the mid-1990s on, they have together created a shared set of sceptical ideas and assumptions about Europe that have permeated the party.

Thereafter, for as long as Britain remained in the EU, Conservative leaders, whether in government or opposition, aspirants for high office, MPs, or candidates in search of constituencies had to take into account the fact that in its bones the party did not like and did not trust Europe. The intensity of this feeling fluctuated over time and in response to the issues at the top of the domestic and European agendas. There were always voices advocating a closer British involvement with the EU, and debate was always possible, but to be pro-European was never the best way to build a successful career.

Would a strong leader with a strong personal commitment to making a success of Britain's membership of the EU have been able to turn the party away from what had become one of its deepest instincts? The answer must be 'probably not', given what happened during the leadership elections that feature in Chapter Seven. The most outstanding of Major's ministers going into the 1997 general election was Ken Clarke. Under his stewardship at the Treasury, the economy was on course to grow faster than those of France and Germany for the sixth successive year, with unemployment down from almost three million to just below two million and inflation running consistently below 3 per cent, except for a brief spike in 1995. Nobody then active in politics could remember a period of such successful economic management. Yet, when he stood for the leadership in 1997, 2001, and

2005, he was on each occasion defeated by men of lesser stature and far more modest achievements than his own because he was regarded as too pro-Europe.

This does not mean that, from the mid-1990s on, Britain was on course to leave the EU. The Conservative Party constituted only one part of the national debate. That aside, if various events to be dealt with in the rest of this book had turned out differently, the In/Out question might never have been put to the people, or at any rate not in the circumstances that it was. It does mean that after the mid-1990s the mind of the Conservative Party and its core voters became increasingly open to the arguments of those, within its own ranks and in other parties, who wanted to take the country out of the EU.

7

Three Leaders 1997–2005

The 1997 general election was a political watershed. It marked the end of eighteen years of Conservative government, the longest continuous period in which any one party has been in power in modern times, and the start of thirteen years of Labour rule. It also marked the moment when Labour picked up the tattered banner of the Party of Europe.

The election was notable for other reasons too. Normally, a government responsible for the kind of economic performance delivered by the Major administration in the years after Black Wednesday could expect to win. That would always have been difficult in 1997, as it would have meant a fifth successive Conservative victory. But, given these very particular circumstances, the government's economic success should, at least, have enabled the party to achieve a respectable result. Instead, it suffered its worst defeat since the Labour landslide of 1945 – a defeat so complete as to banish the party to the periphery of politics.

Labour won 418 seats to the Conservatives' 165, with the Liberal Democrats on 46 and others picking up 29. The Conservative share of the vote was only 30.7 per cent compared with 42 per cent in 1992, and they lost 171 seats. The party was weakened in other ways too. It was left without a single seat in Scotland and Wales, seven Cabinet ministers were defeated, a record number, and a quarter of those who returned to Westminster were newcomers.

The magnitude of the defeat was the result of four factors. Time for a change was one. The Labour Party's programme plus the style, personality, and leadership of Tony Blair was another. The third was 'sleaze', the generic name given to the numerous scandals relating to sex and money that came to characterise the Conservative Parliamentary party in the mid-1990s. The fourth was the extent to which the party appeared to be obsessed by its internal divisions over Europe. The new prime minister joked about this in his first big speech in the House of Commons after his victory. As soon as he began to speak about Europe, Cash and Spicer jumped to their feet to intervene. To the hilarity of the Labour benches, Blair congratulated them and their friends 'on the magnificent part that they played in our victory'.[1]

Besides these headline features, there was another aspect of the 1997 election that would come to have a significant bearing on the Conservative Party's approach to the issue of Europe. It was the first in which rich individuals deployed their own money on a large scale in targeted support of the Eurosceptic cause. Paul Sykes, one of the most successful businessmen in the north of England, did so on an individual basis. Not content with the party's manifesto promise to hold a referendum before any decisions to join the Euro, he offered up to £3,000 to Conservative candidates willing to rule out any possibility of Britain joining it in the next Parliament. An offer which, according to Tim Bale in in his book *The Conservative Party from Thatcher to Cameron*, 'only government members and about 25 pro-Europeans turned down'.[2] Sir James Goldsmith did so by fielding Referendum Party candidates in 547 seats while avoiding those where he regarded the Conservative candidate to be sufficiently anti-EU. He also spent more on press advertising than any other party – £6.8 million compared with £3 million by the Conservatives and £1.5 million by Labour.

In absolute terms, the Referendum Party did badly. Most of

its candidates lost their deposits, and they won only 3.1 per cent of the popular vote in the seats where they stood. Another newcomer to the national scene, the UK Independence Party (UKIP), did even worse with only 1.2 per cent. Even so, it was estimated that their combined effect cost the Conservatives three seats and it could have been much worse. In nineteen others won by the Conservatives, the Conservative majority was less than the Referendum Party's share of the vote, a figure of which the victorious Conservative MPs in those seats would have been acutely aware.

The Referendum Party did not survive Goldsmith's death in July 1997, less than three months after the election, but his influence lived on. UKIP built on the foundations he had laid. Fear that it would launch a challenge in their constituency would constantly prey on the minds of Conservative MPs with modest majorities. They would worry not simply about how many votes a UKIP candidate might collect, but, often and to a greater extent, that some of their own most active supporters might defect to the UKIP cause, thereby blunting their ability to fight against Labour or the Liberal Democrats.

Some Conservatives regarded this not as a threat but as a welcome means of pressuring their own party to cleave to an anti-EU line. When the European Union (Future Relationship) Bill that carried into law the agreement that finally broke Britain's links with the EU was passing through the House of Lords on 30 December 2020, the veteran Conservative Brexiteer Lord Howard of Rising, who as a young man had worked closely with Enoch Powell, said, 'There are very many to whom we must give heartfelt thanks for what they have done to make this agreement possible.'[3] He then singled out Goldsmith and Nigel Farage: the former for having founded the Referendum Party, the latter for the 'ceaseless campaigning' that had helped to bring about the 2016 referendum and later the replacement of Theresa May as prime minister by Boris Johnson.

The combination of circumstances surrounding the 1997 election led the Conservative Party to react to its defeat with none of the wisdom that had characterised its response to past reversals. In 1945 Churchill remained leader of the party when it went into opposition, while Rab Butler on the policy side and Lord Woolton in charge of organisation, both of whom had served in government during the war, undertook the task of rebuilding from the ruins of defeat. So successful were they that in 1950 the party almost returned to power and in 1951 it actually did so. In 1966, as described in Chapter Three, Heath had set in train an ambitious modernisation programme that helped the party to its surprise victory in 1970.

By contrast, in 1997 the election had no sooner ended than the party plunged into a leadership election. The rivalries and disputes that had divided it before the election were resumed. No thorough post-mortem was held into how the party had got into such a mess and no programme established to chart a way out of it. 'We've been in rebellion mode for so long, it's going to be hard to adjust',[4] wrote Michael Spicer in his diary on 4 November 1997, and so it proved. Four leaders followed each other in quick succession. The 2001 election turned out almost as badly as 1997, and the first signs of recovery were not to be seen until the election of 2005.

The reason for this rapid turnover at the top and the electoral failures that flowed from it was what Major had referred to as the 'deep and widening fissure in the party' over Europe.[5] The standout candidate to take over the leadership in 1997 should have been Clarke by virtue of his success as chancellor, his long experience in government, and his popularity with the public at large. Only Heseltine was of comparable political stature, and he had ruled himself out of contention for health reasons. Against that, Clarke was a Europhile and was not prepared to compromise on his support for British entry into the single currency.

If Michael Portillo, the former secretary of state for defence and before that secretary of state for employment, had retained his seat at the recent election, he would have been a highly credible Eurosceptic candidate. The best available alternative was the former home secretary, Michael Howard, who had been an undergraduate contemporary of Clarke's at Cambridge. If, as seemed likely at one point, Howard could have secured the backing of William Hague, he might well have won. As it was, Hague entered the contest as a fresh young face on the Eurosceptic right of the party, while Howard was badly damaged when his former junior minister Anne Widdecombe famously declared that he had 'something of the night about him'.[6] The other candidates were John Redwood, Peter Lilley, and Stephen Dorrell.

If their divisions over Europe had not been so great, MPs might have rallied behind Clarke. As that was impossible, the election went to three rounds, at which point, in an effort to bridge the divisions, Clarke and Redwood formed a pact. They would cooperate on domestic issues under Clarke's leadership while sticking to their positions on Europe and leaving the party's policy open on that subject. The partnership never looked credible and was immediately dubbed a 'marriage from hell'. Nor did it impress Thatcher. Although she barely knew him, she came out publicly for Hague, and he won by ninety votes to Clarke's seventy-two.

Clarke writes in his memoirs that the result was in some ways 'as big a blow to William's career as it was to my own. If I had defeated William in the 1997 leadership election, I would have led the party through five stormy and divided Europe-obsessed years and lost to Tony Blair in 2001. William would have sailed into the leadership in the wake of that defeat and, providing he had opposed the invasion of Iraq, he would probably have defeated a very vulnerable Blair in 2005.'[7] Perhaps. Another scenario is that with the Europe obsession being encouraged by Thatcher in the wings, the party might not have been able to hold together under Clarke.

In personality terms, Hague's most obvious disadvantage when he assumed the leadership was the impression that he and his Shadow Cabinet gave of being a second eleven. He himself had had only two years' experience of Cabinet office as Welsh secretary. Portillo and the other six former Cabinet ministers who had lost their seats were unavailable, while Clarke and Heseltine did not wish to serve. Had they done so, they would have brought gravitas and experience to the team, as Willie Whitelaw, Lord Carrington, and Lord Thorneycroft did when they agreed to serve under the then relatively inexperienced Thatcher in 1975. But for such an arrangement to work, there must be agreement on policy, and on Europe Hague on the one hand and Clarke and Heseltine on the other were poles apart.

After Europe, Hague's biggest problem was how to handle the Thatcherite inheritance. The key to Blair's election victory was his success in convincing the electorate that the Thatcher economic revolution was safe with New Labour. His government would not attempt to turn back the clock. It would run the model created by Thatcher more efficiently and humanely than the Conservatives and give greater priority to the welfare state. It was on this point, and above all education and health, that the Conservatives in opposition had to win back popular support. They had to show that they were not rooted in the 1980s, had learned from their mistakes, and could adapt their fundamental beliefs to contemporary circumstances.

Expressions of hostility to further European integration and to deeper British involvement with the EU would always enthuse the party's rank and file in the constituencies and win plaudits from the Conservative-supporting newspapers. They would very often strike a chord with the wider electorate as well. But they were peripheral to most people's primary political concerns and a distraction from the domestic issues on which the party needed to concentrate. The more that it banged on about Europe, the more it reminded them of the Major government's internal rows and the more it gave the impression of being insufficiently interested in the bread-and-butter questions of domestic politics.

This was the trap Hague set out to avoid. He did so by attempting to close down the internal debate on Europe by committing the party to oppose joining the Euro not just in the present Parliament but in the next one as well, when, it was hoped, the Conservatives would be back in power. The new policy led to the resignation of two talented pro-European members of the Shadow Cabinet, Ian Taylor and David Curry, and provoked the scorn of Clarke and Heseltine: a price thought to be worth paying in return for the overwhelming support of party members. In a ballot, the result of which was announced on the eve of the 1998 party conference, 84 per cent voted in favour. The turnout was disappointingly low at 59 percent of the 350,000 members the party claimed to have on its books, but that was attributed to logistical difficulties and an overestimate of the membership. Few doubted that the result reflected how the mass of the party felt, and the pro-Europeans accepted the verdict.

The Euro was scheduled to be launched in 1999. From the moment Labour won the general election, there was speculation about whether Blair would want Britain to sign up to it. With both parties pledged to hold a referendum before that could be done, the impression gained ground that one might very well take place. It would have suited the Conservatives very well to have fought one on that issue. But it was not to be. Blair had in effect handed the decision over to his chancellor, Gordon Brown. On the basis of five tests he had himself devised, it would be Brown who would determine the decision, which, in practice, meant it would remain in the long grass until after the next election. The result was to create a sense of somehow having been cheated in the minds of all those, by no means only Conservatives, who had been looking forward to a referendum as a means of expressing their view on British engagement in Europe, regardless of the precise subject on the ballot paper.

I was not among those looking forward to such a referendum: quite the reverse, as I knew it would open up a split among those who supported a strong British commitment to the EU. I had supported the opt-out from the single currency secured by Major at Maastricht and had been doubtful from the outset about the wisdom of the Euro project. I did not believe it was in the British interest to sign up to it.[8] Most pro-Europeans wanted to be part of what they saw as a great new initiative from which it would be dangerous for Britain to exclude itself, although a significant minority shared my doubts. Given the unremitting hostility of Eurosceptics to the project, I do not believe that Blair, even at the height of his powers and popularity, could have secured a majority for going in and, in the end, the issue was never put to the test.

Without a referendum to divert it, the party had to concentrate on bringing Thatcherism up to date. As Marxists and Keynesians knew only too well, bringing an 'ism' up to date is difficult to do. Conservatives faced a greater challenge than either of those two groups, because Thatcherism's progenitor, unlike Marx and Keynes, was still very much alive and with ideas of her own about how her legacy should be interpreted.

As a young man without much baggage from the past, Hague was well placed to change the tone of the Conservative message and to rebalance its priorities. In his first party conference speech as leader, in Blackpool in October 1997, he got off to a good start. He talked about Conservatism being about much more than economics, and he stressed the importance of 'obligation to others'. One of his best phrases was that 'freedom doesn't stop at the shop counter',[9] a direct challenge to those in the party who believed that Conservatism meant being liberal on economics and 'small c' conservative on social and 'lifestyle' issues. It was too soon to get into detail on policies, but the direction of travel looked right. He also charged Archie Norman, the former chair and CEO of the Asda supermarket chain and the recently elected MP for Tunbridge Wells, with the task of modernising the Conservative Party organisation. Among the changes Norman introduced was the extension of the franchise for electing the leader from MPs to the whole party membership.

What had started out so promisingly became badly unstuck on 20 April 1999 when the party's deputy leader, Peter Lilley, delivered the annual R. A. Butler Lecture, named in honour of the man who had modernised Conservative philosophy and policies between 1945 and 1950. In a thoughtful speech appropriate to the occasion, Lilley urged Conservatives to 'stop behaving as if we are only true to ourselves when we are applying the market paradigm to anything or everything. It has only a limited role to play in the welfare state'. He warned that because of this attitude there was a widespread belief 'that we are planning to convert public services into profit-making businesses' and denied that this was the intention. Conservatives, he urged, 'must become the champions of better public services'.[10] Throughout the speech, he addressed himself directly to the worries the electorate had about the Conservatives – worries that had to be overcome if the party was ever to return to power. Butler himself would have applauded.

Lilley's colleagues did not. Whether because of the language in which he couched his views, or because of the views themselves, or because they felt they had not been sufficiently consulted and were being bounced, the Shadow Cabinet's reaction was hostile. Press reports that the speech was a repudiation of Thatcherism and that the lady herself had 'gone ballistic' added to the furore.

Within two months, Hague conducted a reshuffle and Lilley was sacked. The net effect of the speech, therefore, was to reinforce the perceptions Lilley had sought to banish and to remind the public that Thatcher – so revered within the party and so widely disliked outside – still exercised a potent influence.

The campaign for the European Parliament elections to be held two months later on 10 June provided the party with the opportunity to put these divisions behind it and to restore unity by reverting to type and going hard on Europe. The election was to be held for the first time on the basis of proportional representation, with the country divided into regions and the parties fielding lists of candidates for each one. An individual candidate's chance of being elected therefore depended on how high he or she was on one of these regional lists. As the party headquarters was responsible for drawing them up, Conservatives holding Eurosceptic if not outright anti-EU views stood a better chance of being in the upper reaches of their lists than those who wanted Britain to join the Euro or who were more enthusiastic about Europe than the leadership. This led to the creation of a rebel Pro-Euro Conservative Party, which, however, proved to be a damp squib.

The core message of the Conservative Party manifesto was 'In Europe, not run by Europe'. It laid great stress on keeping the pound and staying out of the Euro as well as on the preservation of British independence, but it was not a negative document. It made clear that Britain had a long-term commitment to the EU and derived benefit from being a member. It supported the single market, EU environmental protection measures, enlargement to bring in the former communist countries of Eastern Europe, and free movement of people within the EU. It opposed any extension of qualified majority voting, moves towards tax harmonisation, and any idea of a European army.

The tone of the campaign was harsher than the manifesto and

yielded what on the surface appeared to be a dramatic success. The Conservatives doubled their number of seats from eighteen to thirty-six, while Labour was reduced from sixty-two to twenty-nine, but as the turnout was only 24 per cent this was a meaningless guide to what might happen at a general election. Of far greater significance was UKIP's success in winning seats in the European Parliament for the first time, only three, but a start. Proportional representation enabled it to win seats it would never have been able to win on the traditional first-past-the-post system and proved to be the means by which it would become a formidable force in British politics.

UKIP's seats brought with them the additional advantage of a useful stream of income as the party gained access to the Parliament's generous regime of members' expenses and allowances. Thus was created the paradox whereby the European institution most closely identified with the federalist project became a significant financial backer of Britain's principal anti-EU political party. In 2009 the Parliament's contribution would become even more important when it took over the payment of MEPs from the member states and harmonised their salaries at a higher level than that of British MPs, to which British MEPs had hitherto been linked.

The period between the European elections in 1999 and the general election on 7 June 2001 was not a happy one for the Conservative Party. Hague performed well in the House of Commons, often getting the better of Blair at Prime Minister's Questions. The ability to do that can provide a leader of the opposition with the authority and confidence to impose their will on their followers. Thatcher's debating triumphs over Callaghan helped her to achieve that in the 1970s. Hague, however, was unable to prevent a recurrence of the infighting that had so damaged the party under Major, which in turn made it impossible for him to rebuild its reputation for competence. He was equally unsuccessful in finding an effective narrative with which to tackle the government on the welfare state issues that most concerned the electorate.

The former party chair, Lord (Cecil) Parkinson, told Richard Hayton in 2006 that he thought Hague had never had any chance of success:

> Whatever William had done he was never going to appeal to more than the core vote. I couldn't see any floating voters coming back to us after just four years when we'd previously been in power for eighteen ... I think William just decided to go after the core vote because that was the only vote that was likely to come his way.[11]

The rallying cries became 'common sense' and the 'British way', and they involved constantly invoking what was sometimes referred to as the 'Tebbit trinity' of Europe, tax, and immigration.[12]

All three featured prominently in the manifesto for the 2001 general election. As the campaign progressed, Europe played an increasingly prominent role as the party apparently despaired of winning the argument on the NHS, education, and the economy. The pound sign was blazoned over its literature, and as polling day approached the public was warned that only so many days remained 'to save the pound'. As Blair had promised that the country would only join the Euro after a referendum, this claim was clearly absurd and no way to win over floating voters, well though it resonated with those in the party and the press, for whom Europe was an all-consuming interest. The election result was a disaster on a par with 1997. The party made a net gain of only one seat after winning nine and losing eight. Among the new recruits were David Cameron for Douglas Hurd's old seat of Witney (where Hurd's immediate successor, Shaun Woodward, had defected to Labour) and Boris Johnson, who succeeded Heseltine in Henley.

UKIP had caused enough concern before the campaign began for some Conservative candidates to toughen their stance on Europe in return for not having to face a UKIP challenger. In terms of votes and seats it did badly, as in the previous general election. It finished with only 1.5 per cent of the popular vote and 2.1 per cent in the seats it contested, less than the Referendum Party four years earlier and barely a blip on the radar of the major parties. But that was not the whole story. By fielding 428 candidates, it took a big step towards establishing its credentials with the voters as a credible and effective voice of Euroscepticism. A few years later, this would enable it to attract Conservative voters when, as part of his modernisation programme, Cameron tried to tone down the party's Eurosceptic rhetoric.

Another leadership election was an inevitable consequence of the defeat. On 11 June, four days after polling day, Sir Peter Tapsell, with over forty years' experience in the House of Commons, Bill Cash, and Michael Spicer met for lunch at The Athenaeum. They agreed 'that the most likely eurosceptic candidates for the party leadership are Duncan Smith and Davis'.[13] Two men with very different records. As the Europe whip at the time of the Maastricht bill, David Davis had played a prominent role in getting it onto the statute book and then been appointed minister for Europe by Major. Although he had since become well known as a Eurosceptic, there were those who held his past against him. Iain Duncan Smith, by contrast, had been one of the Maastricht rebels who had caused Major so much trouble.

The extension of the franchise to the members of constituency party associations meant that this election would be quite different from any that had gone before. First the MPs would vote in successive rounds until only two candidates were left standing.

Those two would then submit themselves to the verdict of the membership.

The two most experienced and capable candidates were Clarke and Portillo, who was now back in the House. Clarke was the same man as at the previous leadership contest – pro-European, unwilling to compromise on his support for British entry into the Euro, and firmly on the socially liberal wing of the party. By contrast, Portillo had undergone something of a transformation since losing his seat in 1997. While still a Eurosceptic, he had moved across the political spectrum from right to left on social policy. He had also admitted to having had homosexual experiences as a young man. This put him in a double bind. On the one hand, it created huge problems for him with the socially conservative party members. On the other, it provoked the ire of some leading figures in the gay community because he had some years earlier voted against lowering the age of consent for gay men from eighteen to sixteen. The other candidates were Michael Ancram, Davis, and Duncan Smith.

On any conceivable measure of ability and experience, the play off should have been between Clarke and Portillo, and in the first two rounds Ancram and Davis were duly eliminated. In the crucial final round of the Parliamentary party's vote, Clarke came top with fifty-nine votes, but it was Duncan Smith who came second with fifty-four against Portillo's fifty-three. To have to choose between Clarke and Duncan Smith was, in the newly elected Cameron's opinion, 'a hopeless situation. One couldn't unite the party; the other couldn't win over the country'. He opted for Duncan Smith on the grounds 'that if Ken won, the subsequent inevitable party split over Europe would be so bad as to make us both a laughing stock and wide open to a revolt from the right.'[14] In his memoirs, Clarke wondered what would have happened if he and Portillo had gone before the membership: 'the party would have had to choose between two of its more unpalatable prejudices', with the outcome depending on whether it was 'more Europhobic than homophobic or vice-versa'.[15]

As it was, Europhobia – or at least dislike and distrust of the EU – emerged victorious. Despite Clarke's achievements as chancellor and his huge ministerial experience compared with Duncan Smith's lack of any ministerial experience,[16] modest career outside politics, and total lack of charisma, the *Daily Telegraph*, the *Sunday Telegraph*, the *Mail on Sunday* and *The Sun* all came out for Duncan Smith. I backed Clarke, but soon realised that he had no chance. So far as many members were concerned, his credentials were of far less significance than their feeling that Duncan Smith represented their views while Clarke did not. Opinion polls bore this out. They showed that Clarke was four times more popular than Duncan Smith with the public, but that counted for nothing with party members when set against his pro-European view. They voted for Duncan Smith by a margin of 61 per cent to 39 per cent. In a TV interview afterwards, Bill Cash spoke for them when he said, 'The trouble with the 2001 election is that we did not give enough emphasis to the European issue.'[17]

Duncan Smith's weaknesses as a leader were compounded by those of his team. Clarke and Portillo both declined to serve, and not one of those closely associated with the Clarke campaign was given a place in the Shadow Cabinet. Cash became shadow attorney-general, an important appointment in terms of legislation deriving from the EU. Europhiles were present in the lower ranks, but the face of the party was unremittingly Eurosceptic, an impression enhanced in January 2002 when Dominic Cummings, the director of Business for Sterling, an all-party anti-Euro campaign group, was appointed to be the party's Director of Strategy.

Duncan Smith's period as leader did not last long. He had never enjoyed the confidence of the majority of his Parliamentary colleagues, as his share of their vote showed. If he had been able to perform well in the House of Commons, he might have been able to win them over, but in that crucial forum, and especially at Prime Minister's Questions, his performances were dire. Whispering against him soon began to spread across the backbenches. His anti-EU views provided no protection. His demands for loyalty came ill from a man who had made his reputation as a rebel. His efforts to demonstrate concern for the vulnerable and disadvantaged for whom he genuinely felt strongly, as his subsequent career shows, were poorly communicated. His attempts to reach out to women, ethnic minorities, and the gay community failed to secure the backing they deserved.

He also made what turned out to be a massive strategic error by strongly supporting Blair in the run-up to the Iraq War that took place in 2003. This was popular with most Conservative MPs and with the party membership at the time, but later, when the flaws in Blair's case became apparent and public opinion turned against him personally as well as against the war, the Conservatives were unable to derive any electoral benefit from the mess that the government had created for itself.

During 2003 a new force made itself felt when the discontent being expressed by MPs about Duncan Smith's leadership spread to the party's financial backers. In the past, they had not involved themselves in Parliamentary matters. They had been mainly corporates who backed the Conservatives to combat the socialism with which the Labour Party was identified. A combination of New Labour's free-markets agenda and legislative changes inhibiting the ability of companies to make political donations had changed that. The reductions in personal taxation carried through by the Thatcher government and her own popularity with many businesspeople had opened the way for individuals to make large personal donations, both to the party and to pressure groups within it, such as the Eurosceptic

European Research Group. Under Hague, the party had become increasingly dependent on this source of finance, especially from individuals with anti-EU views, who both gave money themselves and raised it from among their friends and connections.

They included three men who served as party treasurer and became members of the House of Lords: Michael Ashcroft, Stanley Kalms, and George Magan. Another was the spread-betting millionaire Stuart Wheeler, who had famously donated £5 million shortly before the 2001 general election and who did not want a peerage. By the autumn of 2003, it was widely known that Ashcroft and Kalms had reduced their support without going public with their criticism. The publicity-loving Wheeler wanted everybody to know his views. After what he considered a poor performance by Duncan Smith at the party conference, he went on the BBC *Today* programme to say 'that it was really essential that Iain Duncan Smith should cease being leader of the Conservative Party'.[18] He flattered himself when he later claimed to have given the 'final push'.[19] A technical problem over the handling of payments to Duncan Smith's wife for work she had undertaken on his behalf did that,[20] but Wheeler's intervention had helped to raise the pressure, and never before in modern times had the party witnessed such an open assertion of money power.

As soon as Duncan Smith lost a vote of no confidence among MPs, Howard telephoned Clarke to ask if he would stand again. Clarke said no. The party had become too right wing and obsessed with Europe. As an enthusiastic pro-European, he felt he had no chance of being elected.[21] Portillo was no longer interested in running, which left only Davis as a possible rival, and he decided not to press his case. Howard was therefore elected unopposed on 6 November 2003.

Given the mood of the party and the balance of forces within it, he was the best choice – a heavyweight political figure with impeccable right-wing credentials. He had held three Cabinet posts under Thatcher and Major and made his name as a tough home secretary, added to which he was a long-standing Euro-sceptic. He was ideally suited to rally the party's core vote. The question was whether he could do that and, at the same time, appeal to the political centre on social and welfare-state issues. Was it possible to please the core vote and the Conservative-supporting newspapers by banging the drum on Europe and replaying the economic and social messages of the Thatcher era while articulating policies that would appeal to middle-of-the-road voters?

As it happened, Howard assumed the Conservative leadership at a moment when the anxieties of those who disliked and distrusted the EU had been brought to a pitch of anxiety. In July 2003 a Convention on the Future of Europe, chaired by the former French president Giscard d'Estaing, had published a draft treaty for the establishment of a Constitution for Europe. Its actual contents, though significant, were a good deal more modest than the document's title implied and fell far short of the work of the American founding fathers, with which Giscard d'Estaing liked to compare them. But both the word 'constitution' and the American allusions were more than enough to set alarm bells ringing in Britain. During the course of 2003 and 2004, as work proceeded on preparing a treaty based on the convention's draft, the Conservatives launched a petition demanding that a referendum should be held before such a treaty could take effect in Britain. Blair responded with a referendum pledge of his own. He then proceeded to sign the treaty at a European Council meeting in Dublin in October 2004.

The referendum pledge was never redeemed. In 2005 the French and Dutch rejected the proposed constitution in national referendums, which killed the treaty. The Luxembourg govern-ment nevertheless went ahead with the one it had planned so that its people could express their opinion, which was in favour. Blair could have given the British people the same opportunity to place their verdict on the record. He decided not to on the grounds that there was no longer any point. Technically he was right, but that did nothing to diminish the resentment felt by those who had for so long wanted to be able to express a view on a European issue. Their hopes of being able to do so on the Euro had earlier been disappointed when, in June 2003, Gordon Brown had announced that, as his five tests had not been met, Britain would not be making an application to join. I think now that it might well have taken a lot of steam out of the European issue if the referendum on the constitutional treaty had been held, although I did not advocate that at the time.

The preparations for the signing of the constitutional treaty provided the backdrop to the European Parliament elections held on 13 June 2004. They also provided the inspiration for the Conservative campaign, which aimed as far as possible to concentrate on European issues. In the manifesto, entitled 'Putting Britain First', opposition to the treaty was centre stage, along with opposition to the Euro. Other points to feature prominently were a demand to get rid of 25 per cent of existing EU regulations and a promise to oppose any harmonisation of immigration, asylum, and border control policies. A statement that 'Conservatives believe Britain cannot and should not turn its back on Europe' was matched by another that 'Conservatives believe Britain should remain an independent state and that our country should not be submerged into a single European state'. In the campaign, this became a promise to keep Britain out of 'a country called Europe'.

Labour adopted a different approach. With local council elections being held on the same day as those for the European Parliament, its aim was to broaden the campaign into a rehearsal of the themes it might run in the general election, likely to take place in 2005. It sought to present Howard as a throwback to Thatcher's poll tax and the party splits of the Major era. Neither the NHS nor the country's education system, Labour asserted, would be safe in his hands. Conservatives, Labour argued, were obsessed by Europe and couldn't be trusted on domestic issues.

In elections in which the fate of the government is not at stake, winning and losing is all about expectations and relative performances. By these criteria, the Liberal Democrats were the big winners in the local elections and UKIP in the European. In the former, the Conservatives came first, but with a lower share of the vote than Hague had achieved when the seats were last contested in 2000, while the Liberal Democrats pushed Labour into third place. In the latter, the Conservatives again came top, but with a smaller share of the popular vote than in 1999 and eight fewer seats at twenty-seven, while Labour lost six to end up with nineteen. UKIP gained ten to finish with twelve, the same as the Liberal Democrats, but with a larger share of the popular vote.

The message to the Conservatives was clear. The UKIP manifesto, entitled 'Better Off Out', encapsulated it. They were now at risk of being outbid in any competition for votes on Europe. They had only themselves to blame, as the former Conservative MEP Ben Patterson explained when he wrote, 'For nearly ten years the message had been that Britain was in danger of being submerged into a "federal super-state" … Many people not surprisingly concluded that we should get out while we could.'[22] In short, UKIP was taking the Conservative message to its logical conclusion.

During the campaign, defections had taken place from the Conservative Party at every level, including five members of the House of Lords, who lost the whip a few days before the poll for urging voters to support UKIP. One was Lord Pearson of Rannoch, a close friend of Thatcher, who recalls that, although she was by then in favour of Britain leaving the EU, he couldn't get her to say so publicly as she didn't want to damage the Conservative Party. She was, however, supportive of him when he left it to join UKIP in 2007 and when he became the UKIP leader in 2010.[23]

Lest anyone might doubt the significance of UKIP's breakthrough, Cash hailed it as 'a historic turning point' and called on the Conservatives 'to move to a fundamental renegotiation of the treaties'.[24] Someone who would play a major role in putting pressure on them to do just that would be Farage, who in 2004 was in charge of UKIP's election committee: an ominous sign of things to come.

The 2004 European Parliament results, though a reliable guide to the underlying movement of public opinion on Europe, did not provide an accurate indicator to what would happen in the general election, called for 5 May 2005. Labour again romped home, though the Conservatives at last had the satisfaction of making up some ground. If they had been able to take advantage of the blame attached to Blair for the Iraq War, they might have done much better, but Howard was as badly placed as his predecessor to do that. As it was, they gained 33 seats to move up to 198 while Labour lost 48 to finish with 355. The Liberal Democrats, who had opposed the war, attracted a lot of disenchanted former Labour voters and gained 11 to move up to 62. UKIP, which had been riven by internal rows, was nowhere to be seen, with a 2.2 per cent share of the national vote.

In terms of how the debate over Europe would develop, the most striking feature of the Conservative campaign was its emphasis on immigration. This was not because of immigration from the Commonwealth as in the days of Enoch Powell, but because of the arrival of large numbers of people from the formerly communist countries of Eastern Europe which had joined the EU in 2004. That enlargement had been the fulfilment of a long-held British ambition. Thatcher had looked forward to it in her Bruges speech. The British hope had been that, just as membership of the EU had helped to bring stability and democracy to Greece, Spain, and Portugal after the fall of their dictatorships, so it would to Eastern Europe. Successive British governments also thought that the more members the EU had, the less likely it would be to develop in a federalist fashion.

What the Blair government failed to take into account was the potential impact of enlargement on immigration into this country. Governments elsewhere in the EU did not make the same mistake. To safeguard the societies and labour markets of Western Europe against the sudden disruption of a sharp increase in immigration after the enlargement, the EU insisted on a transition period, during which the nationals of the new member states would not be allowed to move freely in search of employment in the West until 2011. It was then up to the individual old member states to decide whether or not to avail themselves of this protection. The great majority decided to keep their border closed until the transition period expired. Howard argued that Britain should do the same, but the Labour government, along with the Irish and the Swedes, decided to open them. The effects of this decision were already beginning to be felt in parts of Britain when the general election was called in April 2005.

Lord Adonis, who was head of the Number 10 Policy Unit, and Sir Ivan Rogers, who was the prime minister's principal private secretary when the decision was taken, both recall that it came after 'remarkably little discussion'.[25] The economy was in a strong growth phase with labour shortages appearing, and it was thought that 'Britain would gain a first-mover advantage from tapping into this inexhaustible supply of labour'.[26] The government's forecasters expected that only a few thousand migrants would arrive each year. In fact, more than a million came over four years. In political terms, the benefits that accrued to the economy were soon outweighed by the problems created in some parts of the country for community relations and the social services by the sudden and uncontrolled arrival of so many newcomers. The future Labour Cabinet minister Ed Balls, who was working for Gordon Brown at the Treasury when the decision was taken, has described it as 'a failure of forecasting, of foresight, of politics and understanding' which gave 'rocket boosters to scepticism and hostility towards the EU'.[27] How right he was.

8

Cameron's Dilemmas 2005–2016

Howard had led the Conservative Party to its best general election result since 1992, but there was still a long way to go before it could again become a serious contender for government. To achieve that, a change of generation was required for which the first step was another leadership election. This time, though, there was an interval between the two. Howard remained in situ while a debate took place about whether to introduce new rules for the election of his successor. In the event, no change was made, but the pause provided the party with an invaluable opportunity to reflect on why it was still so far behind Labour and how it might build for the future before the leadership contest was launched at the annual conference at Blackpool in October.

Had the vote for a new leader taken place in the summer, immediately after the general election, Davis would probably have won, and the opportunity to strike out in a new direction would most likely have been lost. By the autumn, the situation looked very different. The realisation that things must change and that the party must broaden its appeal had taken hold, and the beneficiary was Cameron, with his 'Change to Win' slogan. When the conference gathered on 3 October, he was still the outsider. Then, in a bravura speech delivered without notes, he electrified the party members and transformed the situation without winning over most of his Parliamentary colleagues. They recognised his talent, but he had been an MP for only four years, an absurdly short period of time. That, coupled with his gilded background – Eton and private means – and the ease of his ascent aroused mixed emotions.

When the MPs held their first ballot, Cameron came second with fifty-six votes behind Davis on sixty-two and ahead of Liam Fox on forty-two. In last place with thirty-eight came Clarke, still with a loyal band of Europhile and socially liberal followers, inside and outside Parliament, including me, but associated with the past and somewhat out of touch with the new generation of MPs. In the second round, Cameron came top with ninety votes, ahead of Davis on fifty-seven and Fox on fifty-one. Watching the spectacle from the Labour benches, Chris Mullin had no doubt about the significance of what had happened. 'Cameron is now comfortably ahead. Have they recovered the will to win at last?' he wrote in his diary.[1] When the result of the membership ballot was announced, it emerged that he had carried all before him with 134,446 votes to Davis's 64,398.

The reactions in some quarters to Cameron's victory reminded me of Heath's election to the leadership in 1965. There was the same widespread feeling that the party was putting its past behind it, coming to terms with the present, and looking to the future. I hoped it would not prove to be misplaced.

Although a Parliamentary novice, Cameron was in every other respect a quintessential professional politician. At the age of thirty-nine, he had been continuously involved with the Conservative Party since leaving Oxford in 1988, apart from two years in the public relations department of a television company. He had been a special adviser to ministers, an MP, and a shadow minister. He had worked closely with each of the three previous leaders, and especially with Howard, who had promoted him to the Shadow Cabinet. At the time of Black Wednesday, it will be recalled, he had been a special adviser to the then chancellor, Norman Lamont. 'My time at the Treasury,' he writes in his autobiography, 'had made me a Eurorealist or a Eurosceptic.' By this he meant that 'Membership of the EU was necessary for trade and cooperation, but Britain never had and never would welcome the political aspects of the Union.'[2]

Nine months after Cameron's victory, on 12 September 2006, Farage was elected leader of UKIP for the first time. It is salutary to compare their respective attitudes towards the EU. To Cameron, Britain's membership was basically a problem to be managed, which he contended he could do better than anyone else. To Farage, that problem was best dealt with by the simple expedient of withdrawal. UKIP would ceaselessly plug that message while Cameron, initially as leader of the opposition and, from 2010, as prime minister, would grumble and complain about the EU and call for its reform, but rarely say a word in its favour. He never made a clear and convincing case for staying in, with the result that over time it was Farage, UKIP, and those who thought like them who came to dictate the terms of the argument on the centre-right and right wing of British politics.

During his campaign for the party leadership, Cameron provided proof of his Eurosceptic credentials when he promised to withdraw the Conservatives in the European Parliament from the EPP. In 1992 the Conservative MEPs had finally been permitted by the party leadership to team up with the other centre-right groups by joining this Christian Democrat-led grouping, mainly because doing so would give them more influence in the Parliament's affairs than remaining outside. From the outset, hard-line Conservative Eurosceptics had objected to this arrangement on the grounds that the Christian Democrats were too federalist. After the 1999 European elections, the newly elected Daniel Hannan[3] created something of a stir by threatening to refuse to sit with them for that reason. The row over the relationship rumbled on during the Hague, Duncan Smith, and Howard years. Cameron's promise to withdraw helped him to win over the support of right-wingers and Eurosceptics who might otherwise have preferred Davis or Fox, although there can be little doubt that he would have won anyway. Spicer described it in his diary as 'DC's one major promise during his election campaign'.[4]

Cameron subsequently claimed that by promising to withdraw from the EPP he was getting away 'from the "doublespeak" of the past' and taking 'a clear and consistent' stand against federalism.[5] What he overlooked, or did not at the time understand, was that the EPP had become something much more significant than a grouping of MEPs in the European Parliament. It had become a pan-European network of centre-right political parties involving not only MEPs but also national politicians and their party leaders, whether in government or opposition.

It was where ideas were exchanged, friendships formed, common approaches hammered out, and deals done, including by heads of government before meetings of the European Council. In announcing his intention to withdraw while running for the leadership of his party, Cameron excluded himself from their deliberations and from the personal relationships to which they gave rise when he became prime minister. To what extent this self-exclusion put him at a disadvantage is, in the nature of things, impossible to calculate. It certainly did so on two occasions. One was in 2011, when the German chancellor, Angela Merkel, and the French president, Nicolas Sarkozy, hatched a plan at a meeting of EPP leaders to circumvent a veto they expected him to impose at a forthcoming meeting of the European Council. The other was in 2014, when, as a result of machinations within the EPP, he was first blind-sided and then voted down over the nomination of Jean-Claude Juncker to become president of the Commission.

Having established his credentials on Europe with the sceptics in his party during his leadership campaign, Cameron wanted to put the whole question on to the backburner. And not just Europe. He wanted to downplay tax, immigration, and crime as well: all the issues that appealed to the Conservative core vote and to the right-wing newspapers and which UKIP stood ready to take over. In his speech to the 2005 party conference, he singled out for mention the need for high-quality, properly funded public services, thereby indicating this as one of the battlegrounds on which he wanted to take the fight to Labour. He also identified himself with the environment and climate change. International development, women's issues, and the concerns of ethnic minorities also moved sharply up the Conservative agenda. The aim, in advertising terms, was to 'decontaminate' the brand and to show that the party was focusing on the contemporary issues that Blair had made his own rather than constantly re-fighting the battles of the past.

This was the right decision for a party wanting to win back power. For those with long memories, it was reminiscent of Heath's modernisation programme and preparations for government in the late 1960s, with two big differences. Cameron went about his task with a great deal more charm than Heath, while, in Heath's case, active British participation in the EEC, as it then was, had been an integral part of his project.

For Cameron, arguments over Europe were part of the baggage of the past. Two speeches encapsulated his approach. In his opening address to the 2006 party conference in Bournemouth, he told the delegates, 'While parents were worried about childcare, getting the kids to school, balancing work and family life – we were banging on about Europe.'[6] This followed a speech a few months earlier to the Conservative Spring Forum in which he had characterised UKIP as 'a bunch of fruitcakes and loonies and closet racists'.[7] In the context of his decontamination project, his party conference speech made sense as an attempt to show that the party was now concerned with issues that worried ordinary people rather than those with which it had, up till then, been identified. Likewise, his dismissal of UKIP was an attempt to distance the party from those who banged on most loudly about Europe and to discourage Conservatives from associating with them. In fact, because the words he used were so disdainful and so redolent of an 'upper-class toff' referring to his social inferiors, it had the reverse effect. It showed, too, how much he underestimated UKIP's potential and the campaigning abilities of Farage.

The great set piece of any Conservative annual conference is the leader's closing speech. When Cameron delivered his in Bournemouth in 2006, he made no mention of Europe, the clearest possible indication that he did not want the party to dwell on it. The problem was that Europe could not be shunted off to one side as if it was yesterday's issue. The management of the EU's existing policy areas – the single market, international trade, agriculture, the Eurozone, etc – continually generated new proposals to which the government had to respond and on which the opposition had to take a view. The two issues demanding most attention in Cameron's early years were the consequences of the 2008 financial crash on the Eurozone and the flow of migrants into Britain from the EU and into the EU from Africa and the Middle East.

That aside, deep-seated fears about the nature of Britain's relationship with the EU and its perceived threat to national sovereignty persisted among the Conservative membership and a significant proportion of the wider electorate. Europe was often low on the list of voters' concerns as interpreted by the pollsters, but, however dormant it appeared to be, like embers in a grate, the fears surrounding it could at any moment be fanned into flames. Conservative leaders had for many years been feeding those fears. Just because they stopped doing so, the fears would not go away, and UKIP stood ready to nourish them. In taking on that role, it would not necessarily win many votes for itself, except in elections to the European Parliament, but it would exert a magnetic attraction on core Conservative supporters and thus put pressure on Conservative MPs fearful for their majorities.

As Cameron wished Britain to remain in the EU, he should not simply have tried to stop the party from banging on about it in the old way. He should have developed a case to convince people of the merits of membership in terms of British interests, shared values like those underpinning the relationship with the United States, and a vision of the sort of Europe he would like to see and Britain's role within it. He failed to attempt this until far too late, by which time his argument for staying in failed to carry conviction.

During their years in opposition from 2005 to 2010, Cameron and his team achieved great success both at decontaminating the Conservative brand and at becoming credible exponents of economic and social policies that appealed to the wider electorate. By winning over a broad swathe of electors who had previously been attracted to Blair, the Conservatives were able to become the largest single party in the House of Commons at the 2010 general election and to achieve an overall majority in 2015. The payback for failing to develop a good case for staying in the EU came in the 2016 referendum. When Cameron campaigned to remain, his efforts to present it in a positive light sounded unconvincing by comparison with what he had said in the past. As his deputy chief of staff, Kate Fall, so aptly put it when describing his difficulties during the referendum campaign, 'We had never rolled the pitch for Britain staying in Europe.'[8] Those who had never stopped banging their drum for coming out reaped their reward for not giving up.

The writing was on the wall as early as the opening weeks of 2007, when the ConservativeHome website reported that UKIP was the second-favourite party of nearly half of all Conservative members. This was not just because of Europe. It also stemmed from Farage's determination to broaden his party's appeal to those who were put off by Cameron's brand of liberal conservatism, liked the way the Conservative Party had differentiated itself from Blair, and disliked the attempt to take over his territory. They objected to Cameron's failure to support grammar schools and his embrace of such causes as climate change and international development. They wanted him to continue his predecessors' emphasis on tax cuts, reducing immigration, and Europe. When in 2013 Cameron carried a bill through Parliament to legalise same-sex marriage, they were appalled.

Second favourite did not mean they would necessarily abscond, though some did so over same-sex marriage. It did mean that they were willing on occasion, like in elections to the European Parliament, to lend their votes to UKIP, and that they would seek to persuade their Conservative MP or the candidate in their constituency to adopt UKIP positions. The same was equally true of others who were not party members but usually voted Conservative. It meant that if ever Europe should become the central issue in the political battle, as it would in a referendum, Cameron would find it difficult to hold onto their votes.

He was fortunate to have five years in which to re-position his party. In 2007, after Brown had succeeded Blair as prime minister on 27 June, the government enjoyed the kind of bounce in the polls that often comes with a change at the top. In July Labour outpolled the Conservatives on all issues about which people were questioned except immigration. In September it averaged 40 per cent, with a lead over the Conservatives of 5 to 6 per cent. There was talk of the forthcoming Conservative conference in Blackpool being Cameron's second and last, and the acronym PODWAS, standing for Poor Old Dave What a Shame, briefly entered into circulation.

Brown was widely expected to call a general election to secure a mandate of his own rather than continuing to live off Blair's. As the autumn conference season approached, and the government allowed the speculation to gather momentum until it seemed as if the only question was when rather than whether there would be an election, Cameron and his team were desperately finalising their battle plans. When Labour's conference passed without an announcement, the Conservatives were able to hold a very successful one of their own, the highlight being an announcement by George Osborne, the shadow chancellor, that under a Conservative government only estates of over £1 million would be subject to inheritance tax.

In the immediate aftermath of the conferences, polling in marginal constituencies showed a swing away from the government, and Brown pulled back from the election edge to hoots of Conservative derision about being afraid and 'bottling it'. In financial terms, it was an expensive withdrawal, as Labour had pre-paid £1.2 million for poster sites, which were then not used. In political terms, the cost to Brown's reputation was much greater.

What the result of an election would have been is hard to say. What I am sure of is that the country was fortunate to have had the experienced team of Brown and his chancellor, Alistair Darling, in charge when the world financial crisis erupted in the autumn of 2008. They dealt with it extremely competently, with Brown playing a more substantial role on the international stage than any British prime minister has done since. It is difficult to believe that the inexperienced Cameron and Osborne would have fared nearly as well. Inevitably, however, the consequences for the domestic economy and the national finances were unpleasant. They took a heavy toll on the government's popularity in 2009, and, during the 2010 election campaign, the Conservatives succeeded, most unfairly, in pinning the blame on Brown personally.

Another problem Brown had to contend with as a result of

continuing in government was a new EU proposal that came to be known as the Lisbon Treaty. After the rejection of Giscard d'Estaing's European Constitution, the member states had agreed on a new treaty that incorporated the central elements of the constitution while eschewing the pretentious language with which he had clothed them. The deal was concluded in the final days of Blair's premiership. Brown accepted it, but he did not revive the government's earlier promise of a referendum on the grounds that that promise had applied only to the original constitutional treaty and was not applicable to its replacement, an explanation that was widely regarded as a breach of faith.

Cameron saw an opportunity. By opposing the bill to ratify the Lisbon Treaty in Parliament and promising that, once elected to government, he would call a referendum on it, he could have his cake and eat it. He could fight a battle on Europe that would please Eurosceptics and outright anti-Europeans while justifying it to middle-of-the-road electors on the grounds of Labour's broken promise. However, he added the important caveat that a referendum would not be possible if, by the time the Conservatives won the election, the treaty had already been ratified by all the other member states and therefore had become law. In the event, this is exactly what happened. Thus, yet another referendum promise was unfulfilled.

But this is to jump ahead. Before the general election could take place in 2010, elections to the European Parliament had to be held in 2009. In March of that year, Stuart Wheeler, the man who had given £5 million to Hague before the 2001 general election, presented UKIP with a cheque for £100,000 with, he later claimed, the blessing of Norman Tebbit.[9] He was duly expelled from the Conservative Party. Welcome though he and his money were to UKIP, the party looked to be heading for a disappointing election until they were saved by a political earthquake in the form of the scandal over MPs' expenses. It broke just as campaigning was getting under way and did enormous damage to the reputations of Parliamentarians of all parties. Cameron was widely judged to have handled the revelations involving Conservative MPs better than Brown with Labour's, but, as far as most electors were concerned, all mainstream political figures were tarred by the same brush.

Nothing could have suited UKIP better. Without any MPs of its own, it was ideally placed to benefit from the national disillusionment with the major parties. All the work it had done to widen its support base and to improve its organisation was given a massive boost. At the same time, its anti-immigration message and unsubstantiated assertions that EU membership was costing Britain £40 million a day acquired a new resonance. It still did less well than it had hoped, with a gain of only one seat to move up to thirteen, way behind the Conservatives' twenty-six, but, because it won the same number of seats as Labour and a higher percentage share of the vote, it was able to claim a famous victory. The extent of its gains among blue-collar voters and in the North-East, North-West, and Yorkshire was a harbinger of things to come in the 2016 referendum. Farage chose this moment to stand down from the leadership in order to concentrate on becoming MP for Buckingham in the forthcoming general election. His successor, Lord Pearson of Rannoch, had none of his flair nor his ability to overcome the infighting to which the party was prone.

When the general election was held on 6 May 2010, the Conservatives achieved a similar swing to that which had brought Margaret Thatcher to power in 1979. But, in the new era of multi-party politics, with the Liberal Democrats and the SNP playing larger roles than in her day, it was not enough to secure an overall majority. With 306 seats, a gain of 96, they were well ahead of Labour on 258, but 20 short of an overall majority. Although the Liberal Democrats lost 5 seats, the 57 they won were sufficient to give them the balance of power in the House of Commons, the fulfilment of an age-old dream. Cameron immediately invited them to join a coalition. After a brief flirtation with Brown, their leader, Nick Clegg, accepted. A surprisingly brisk negotiation between representatives of the two leaders then resulted in a Coalition Agreement followed by the formation of Britain's first coalition government since the war.

No two parties disagreed more about the EU than the Conservatives and the Liberal Democrats. As Oliver Letwin, one of the Conservative negotiators of the Coalition Agreement, later put it, his colleagues 'ranged from nascent "Euro-outers" through strong Eurosceptics to milder Eurosceptics whereas the Liberal Democrats around the cabinet table were mainly people whose political formation was bound up with belief in the EU'.[10] While some Conservatives wanted no more integration and others wanted to undo what there was, the Liberal Democrats were united in their desire for Britain to become more deeply embedded in the EU.

Despite these differences, the two parties had one crucial commitment in common. Both had fought the election with a manifesto commitment to hold a referendum before any further deepening of Britain's relationship with the EU could take place. The Liberal Democrats' manifesto stated that they were 'committed to an In/Out referendum the next time a British government signs up to a fundamental change in the relationship between the UK and the EU'. It also stated that 'Britain should join the Euro only if that decision were supported by the people of Britain in a referendum'. The Conservative manifesto undertook to 'ensure that by law no future government can hand over areas of power to the EU or join the Euro without a referendum of the British people'. It further promised that 'a Conservative government will never take the UK into the Euro'.

Thanks to these commitments, it was relatively easy for the

two parties' negotiating teams to agree that there would be no further transfer of sovereignty in the present Parliament, that the EU's current competencies would be subjected to an examination, and that any proposed future treaty requiring a transfer of powers would require a referendum. With so many commitments to a referendum being thrown around, it was becoming inevitable that sooner or later one would have to be held, though whether In/Out or on some narrower issue remained to be seen.

Conservative MPs and voters were delighted to see their party back in government, but because it was in coalition with the Liberal Democrats the new government's centre of gravity was more centrist and liberal than if Cameron and his team had been governing alone, and markedly more so than the Parliamentary Conservative Party as a whole. This was naturally a matter of deep concern to those MPs who felt they were being pushed to the fringes, and particularly to those individuals who believed they had been denied a ministerial post to make room for the Liberal Democrat appointments. Consequently, declarations of independence by individual MPs wanting to make a name for themselves, expressions of discontent with government policy, and backbench rebellions were all likely to come from the right and to focus on issues of concern to the right.

Of these the most obvious was Europe. It was fraught enough in itself, but, when linked to immigration and other questions that in 2007 had already made UKIP the second-favourite party of Conservative members, its disruptive potential was greatly increased. With Farage resuming the leadership of UKIP in November 2010, after failing to become an MP, he and his party stood ready to take advantage of the opportunities the coalition presented.

They had two other advantages. One was that, as part of the governing coalition, the Liberal Democrats could no longer fulfil their traditional role as the depository for protest votes, thereby clearing the way for UKIP to take it over. The other was the rising public concern over immigration by EU nationals and others from the Commonwealth and elsewhere into the UK. On this issue, Cameron had become a dangerous hostage to fortune. In January 2010, he had promised to reduce the net rate[11] from all sources, then running at around 200,000 a year, to the tens of thousands. This pledge, which his government never came anywhere near meeting, would come back to haunt him in all future electoral contests and, most damagingly, during the referendum campaign.

Farage seized his chance. At his party's spring conference in March 2011, he declared, 'No longer is UKIP on the fringes of any national debate. We are right on the centre ground of public opinion in this country.'[12] An exaggeration, perhaps, at the time when he uttered those words, but, with at least one opinion poll already putting UKIP ahead of the Liberal Democrats, by no means unjustified. As a third party, the Liberal Democrats had often found it hard to raise money. UKIP was more fortunate. Wheeler agreed to become the party's treasurer and set about soliciting contributions, including, on terms of anonymity, 'from those prominent Conservative supporters who also happened to believe very strongly that we should leave the EU'.[13]

This combination of factors placed Cameron in an awkward position. UKIP's aim was clear. It wanted Britain out of the EU. A large section of the Conservative Party, both in Parliament and in the constituencies, was to a greater or lesser degree attracted to that position. He was in favour of staying, but as a Eurosceptic himself he had failed to construct a compelling case for doing so. Instead of being able to argue with the leavers in terms of British interests, enhancing British influence, and shared values with our partners, he offered an unconvincing mix of his own Eurosceptic language and an endless vista of crisis management, arguments with the Commission and other member states, and technical compromises that few would understand. He did not even have an explanation of the costs and complexities of leaving against which to measure the arguments of those who wished to take Britain out.

Nor could he move Europe onto the backburner as he had once hoped. The increasing flow of immigrants from Eastern Europe into this country and from the Middle East and Africa into the EU made that impossible. So, too, did the impact of the financial crisis on the finances of the weaker members of the Eurozone and the consequential threats posed to the survival of the Eurozone itself. These in turn necessitated treaty adjustments that required the unanimous approval of all EU member states, whether part of the Eurozone or not. Europe, in short, was rarely out of the news, and Parliament was constantly being called upon to approve measures relating to it.

As soon as it took office after the May 2010 general election, the government set about redeeming Cameron's manifesto promise to legislate for an automatic referendum on any proposal to transfer significant further powers to the EU. This was welcomed by his supporters but did nothing to deter them from asking for more. The first Conservative backbench rebellion on Europe came in October, on the House of Commons' return from the long summer recess. In a debate on the EU budget, thirty-seven MPs defied a three-line whip by joining Labour in demanding a cut in the UK contribution. It set a precedent for the future. Over the following year, the habit of rebellion became ingrained as a further twenty-one took place involving some sixty MPs.

This rebellious habit set the scene for a major confrontation in October 2011, when the House of Commons debated a backbench motion on a public petition calling for an In/Out referendum that had attracted 100,000 signatures. A backbench motion is not binding on the government, but, if Labour had abstained on this one and if it had been carried by Conservative votes, the government would have been boxed in. If there was to be such a referendum, Cameron wanted it to be on terms and at a time of his own choosing, not to have it forced on him by his own backbenchers. The whips therefore mounted a major operation to defeat it. They succeeded, but with eighty-one MPs defying them, including forty-nine from the newly elected 2010 intake, it was the most pyrrhic of victories. Cameron was shocked and felt that 'it showed the extent to which the ground was moving beneath us'.[14]

The pyrrhic victory at Westminster was followed by another, even more pyrrhic, at the European Council meeting at Brussels on 8 and 9 December 2011. While the Westminster battle was being fought, EU ministers and diplomats were putting together a plan for a so-called fiscal compact to strengthen the Eurozone. As it touched on the interests of the City of London, Cameron decided that, since it was a treaty change requiring the unanimous approval of all member states, he would seize the opportunity to push through various proposals to benefit the City – in other words, to use what he saw as leverage over the Eurozone as a means of furthering British interests. In the days preceding the Council, British officials let it be known that he was willing to veto the plan if he did not get his way. Other member states were furious, believing that he was putting British interests that could be pursued by other means ahead of a measure urgently needed to save the Eurozone.

At this point, Merkel and Sarkozy, at a pre-Council meeting of EPP heads of government, hatched a plan to outflank him. If he went ahead with his veto, they would table a new plan for an intergovernmental fiscal compact treaty outside the framework of the EU treaties. Not until the Council meeting began to stretch into the night did Cameron become aware of what was afoot and that the other leaders had all been squared. Eventually, at 2:30 a.m., he imposed his veto, the first ever by a British prime minister, thereby killing the original proposal. The other leaders promptly went ahead without him by activating the Merkel–Sarkozy plan. Far from having stopped the EU in its tracks, as he had intended, Cameron was left looking isolated and impotent among his peers in Brussels.

In London, his own MPs and supporters welcomed him back as a conquering hero. What mattered to them was that a proposed EU treaty had been blocked by the British prime minister, not that the other member states had found a way of proceeding without Britain. The Mayor of London and former *Daily Telegraph* Brussels correspondent, Boris Johnson, congratulated him on having 'played a blinder'.[15] The very fact of his isolation played to Cameron's advantage. As the Conservative pollster Andrew Cooper[16] later explained, 'The more the BBC stress how isolated Britain was and how it was twenty-five in the EU against Britain, the better it played for us. Our focus groups liked Cameron standing up for his country and saying "no" to the EU.'[17] Another factor that pleased Conservatives was the fury of the Liberal Democrats and their frustration at not having been able to prevent Cameron's action.

When the 1922 Committee met the following week, Cash declared, 'The fact that we're now vetoing this treaty means that we are set on a path which involves fundamental renegotiation. Make no mistake about that.'[18] He was right.

Cameron was under no illusion about what had happened in Brussels. The experience had shown him that the veto was not the impregnable defensive shield he had thought it was. Another revelation was how determined the Eurozone member states were to save their project, one that with them would always take priority over his conception of British interests. There was no question in his mind of aligning British interests more closely with theirs, let alone contemplating the possibility of joining the

Euro. Quite the reverse: he was becoming increasingly worried by the destructive force of the Europe issue within the Conservative Party and, though he was loath to admit it, the drift of Conservative supporters in the country towards UKIP. As he reflected on these matters over Christmas, he found himself, by January 2012, increasingly drawn to the idea of 'at some stage altering Britain's relationship with the European Union in some regards and then putting it to a referendum'.[19]

While Cameron cogitated on these matters, pressure was building up on another front following the European Court of Human Rights (ECHR) ruling that the home secretary, Theresa May, could not deport the terrorist suspect Abu Qatada to Jordan. The ECHR has no connection with the EU,[20] but the sight of another international institution with the word 'European' in its name overruling the British government on such a matter added a further layer of toxicity to the debates over sovereignty and immigration.

Immigration, both in terms of EU citizens coming to Britain and refugees from Africa and the Middle East entering the EU, was never far from the headlines during 2012. The impact of the financial crisis on the Eurozone and particularly the hardships suffered by Greece also received widespread coverage. Both strengthened the hands of the Eurosceptics. UKIP benefitted accordingly, as well as from its own improved organisation and the mix of policies that it offered. During 2012 it often outstripped the Liberal Democrats in the opinion polls. Another more tangible sign of its growing strength was the number of candidates it was fielding in local elections, up from 323 in 2006 to over 1,000 in 2011. In May 2012 it averaged 13 per cent of the vote in the seats it contested, 5 points up on the previous year thanks in large part to Conservative defections. The Conservative MP Gary Streeter warned, 'The UKIP vote is not just about Europe. It's also about a hard core of traditional Conservative voters saying, actually we don't like the kind of small-l liberal decisions this government is beginning to take. It offends us and we're going to protest and vote UKIP.'[21]

In November, the UKIP challenge looked even more formidable when, at the Corby by-election, the UKIP candidate won 14.3 per cent of the vote, its highest ever in a Parliamentary by-election, with the Liberal Democrats losing their deposit. Two weeks later at Rotherham, the party did even better, coming second with 21.7 per cent, ahead of the Conservatives as well as the Liberal Democrats. In these seats, many of its new voters were traditional Labour supporters, but this did nothing to diminish the Conservative fear that the more success UKIP achieved, the harder it would be for Conservatives to win an overall majority at the next election.

Under the pressure of these events, Cameron was not the only Conservative to be attracted by the idea of a referendum. In June, 100 MPs signed a letter demanding that legislation should be brought forward to enable one to be held after the next general election. With few exceptions, those rooting for a referendum wanted one because they thought it would result in Britain leaving the EU. Those around Cameron took a contrary view. They shared his emerging view that, if he could alter Britain's relationship with the EU, he would be able to win and thus bring the party's internecine war over Europe to an end. George Osborne seems to have been the only person to have warned against going down this road, on the grounds that the battle might be lost, and what then would happen? A different argument was put by Andrew Mitchell during his brief period as chief whip in autumn 2012. He recalls advising along the lines of 'You won't lose, but you should not do this. You would be using a national referendum to resolve what is essentially a party political issue.'[22]

In October, another rebellion took place in the House of

Commons when fifty-three MPs defied a three-line whip to join Labour to defeat the government on an amendment demanding a cut in the overall limit to be set on the EU budget for the next quinquennium. Some months later, when the government was actually able to achieve this as one of a majority of member states that cut back the Commission's plans, its success was barely noticed in Britain.

Significant for the future though these events were, Europe was not by any means at the forefront of political debate in 2012. The issues that attracted most attention were the priority attached by the government to reducing the public sector deficit, the impact on the public services of its austerity programme to achieve that, and the consequences of a botched reform of the NHS. The government was on the wrong side of public opinion on all three, but, so far as the public was concerned, by far the most important events of the year had nothing to do with politics. They were the Queen's Diamond Jubilee celebrations and the London Olympic Games. Each was superbly organised and a great success. Together they did much to make the country forget about politics and feel good about itself.

As the end of the year approached and the feel-good factor began to wane, Cameron decided to go for a referendum to be held before 2017, if the Conservatives won the next general election, scheduled for 2015. Work was set in train on the speech he would make to announce his decision, which was delivered on 23 January 2013 at the London headquarters of Bloomberg, the American-owned media, data analysis, and software company. Given its importance, the speech was prepared in unusual circumstances. Normally a prime ministerial pronouncement on a major policy matter would at the very least benefit from civil service input and quite likely be written by civil servants. That could not happen in this case. In committing himself to hold a referendum, Cameron was not speaking for the government. He was speaking only for the Conservatives within it. He therefore had to rely on his core team of Conservative special advisers.

Cameron was in no doubt about the significance of what became known as the Bloomberg speech. In his autobiography, he describes it as 'probably the biggest speech of my career'. He saw it at the time as one that 'could change my country and the continent forever'.[23] During the course of it, he came closer than he ever had before to articulating a vison of the EU and Britain's role within it, and he did so in strikingly pro-European terms. Clarke, now a member of the Cabinet as minister without portfolio, was 'pleasantly surprised'.[24] Others, accustomed to his usual Eurosceptic rhetoric, were correspondingly shocked. They had not been prepared for this change of tone.

The speech dealt at some length with what Cameron believed was wrong with the EU in its current form, changes he would like to see implemented, and why he hoped that if those changes were made Britain would vote to remain a member. Two features stand out. One is the importance he attached to securing formal recognition of British exceptionalism and the significance of his proposed reforms of the EU and its working methods.

The other, as the former British permanent representative to the EU and EU adviser to Blair, Sir Stephen Wall, has pointed out in his book *The Reluctant European*, is the contrast between Cameron's approach in 2013 and Wilson's and Callaghan's in 1975:

> Their position was that they would only decide what recommendation to make once the re-negotiation of the terms of UK membership had been completed ... Cameron by contrast came close to saying that EU membership was of overriding importance to the UK, a sure way of de-valuing his negotiation credentials with his own Eurosceptics and with the EU partners from whom he would have to wring concessions.[25]

I would go further. When Cameron said, 'I believe something very deeply. That Britain's national interest is best in a flexible, adaptable, and open European Union, and that such a European Union is best with Britain in it,'[26] he was clearly committing himself to keeping Britain in the EU if he could.

Wall's point was not the only difference between the Cameron and Wilson negotiating positions. As explained in Chapter Four, Wilson took care to avoid issues he thought would not interest the British people, notably the budget, and concentrated on what he judged, rightly as it turned out, would play well with them if he succeeded, namely enhanced access for Commonwealth foodstuffs. Cameron could not do that. When he launched his re-negotiation, the most sensitive Europe-related matter in the minds of the British people and the one bound to attract a disproportionate amount of attention in their assessment of whatever deal he secured was immigration. They wanted to see a mechanism for controlling the number of migrants entering this country from the EU and elsewhere and a sharp reduction in those numbers. They also wanted an end to the ECHR over-ruling British ministers on deportation matters. Yet there was little Cameron could do to deliver on either. Freedom of move-ment was a fundamental principle of the EU which, now that the transition period foregone by Blair had expired, it would be very difficult to change. Furthermore, the ECHR had nothing to do with the EU and was outside the scope of the negotiation.

Cameron's hope that his referendum pledge would blunt UKIP's challenge in the country and put a stop to the constant agitation of his hard-line Eurosceptic backbenchers in the House of Commons was soon disappointed.

The first test of UKIP's strength came just a month after the Bloomberg speech, at a by-election at Eastleigh in Hampshire triggered by the resignation of the Liberal Democrat Cabinet minister Chris Huhne. Though the Liberal Democrats held the seat with 32.5 per cent of the vote, UKIP came second, pushing the Conservatives into third place with Labour fourth. Two months later, UKIP again did well, this time in the safe Labour seat of South Shields near Newcastle. Labour won easily with over 50 per cent of the vote while UKIP were again runners up with 24.2 percent, more than twice that of the Conservatives in third place. A pattern was thereby established. Whether in the south of England or the north, UKIP had become the principal challenger to the incumbent party, not the Conservatives or Labour.

Trouble came in the House of Commons with the Queen's Speech in May, when over 114 Conservatives supported an amendment regretting that the referendum pledge had not been included in the government's current legislative programme. This was a thoroughly unreasonable position as there was no chance of the Liberal Democrats agreeing to such a proposal, but a very effective way of demonstrating the strength of feeling on the backbenches.

Further embarrassment quickly followed when James Wharton,[27] one of the 114, was successful in the ballot for Private Members' bills and tabled one to legislate immediately for a referendum. In any remotely normal circumstances, the government would have left it to die a natural death like most Private Members' bills. Cameron, however, was by this time so anxious to regain control of what had become a runaway train that he jumped into the driver's seat by ordering all Conservatives to vote for Wharton's bill on a three-line whip.[28] As there was no Conservative majority in either the House of Commons or the House of Lords, the bill was inevitably defeated. The prime minister and his ministerial colleagues were thus left in the absurd position of having voted for a measure the coalition government of which they were a part refused to accept. In mitigation, they could say that by doing so they had shown how serious they were about implementing Cameron's promise to hold a referendum if they won the next general election.

Before the Fixed Term Parliaments Act, enacted by the coalition government in 2011, Cameron would have been free to go to the country on a date he thought most advantageous to his party. In the new circumstances created by the act, the election had to be held on 7 May 2015. As a result, there was no way he could avoid a prior clash with UKIP in the 2014 elections to the European Parliament. In the light of previous UKIP successes in European elections and the recent by-elections, it was almost inevitable that 2014 would be a bonanza for the party, and so it turned out.

When the polls closed on 24 May, UKIP emerged triumphant. With twenty-four seats, it became the leading British party in the Parliament ahead of Labour on twenty and the Conservatives on nineteen, the first time since 1910 that a party other than the Conservatives or Labour had won the largest number of seats in a national election. As the turnout was only 35.8 percent, this result could not be taken as a reliable indicator of what might happen in a general election. But it did amply demonstrate how strong UKIP had become when Europe was at the centre of the debate, as it would be in Cameron's promised referendum, and how, on that issue, it could appeal to both Conservative and Labour supporters.

In Britain, the European election was fought without regard to what was happening elsewhere in the EU. In other, but not all, member states, the terms of engagement were quite different. The main pan-European groups represented in the European Parliament – the EPP, Socialists, Liberals – had agreed to press the heads of government to accept the candidate of whichever party finished top of the poll across the EU as the next president of the Commission. As the EPP came top, this meant that the Luxembourg prime minister Jean-Claude Juncker became the Parliament's nominee.

He was the one Cameron least wanted and had lobbied most actively against. Merkel had not wanted him either, and Cameron thought he had an undertaking from her that she would use her influence with the Christian Democratic Union of Germany, the largest national contingent in the EPP, to block the nomination. To his surprise, she did not deliver. This was not because of bad faith on her part. It was because her party members felt so strongly on the matter that she felt unable to stand out against them. As a result, when the European Council met on 27 June, she supported Juncker and Cameron suffered a public defeat. If he had not excluded himself and his party from the EPP, he might have been able to exert some influence on its choice of candidate and would not have been caught out in the way that he was.

At home, further blows followed. In August, the Conservative MP for Clacton, Douglas Carswell, defected to UKIP, and in September, Mark Reckless, the MP for Rochester and Strood, followed him. Both then resigned from the House of Commons, which they were not obliged to do. Standing as UKIP candidates, they then won back their constituencies at the subsequent by-elections in October and November. Immigration, and the government's failure to get anywhere near its 'tens of thousands' target, had been very much at the centre of the political debate during the months leading up to the defections and worked powerfully in UKIP's favour at the by-elections. In fact, for many who voted UKIP, the control and reduction of immigration had become their main priority, with leaving the EU the means of achieving it.

Cameron sought to meet these concerns with a big speech on limiting immigration from within the EU, which he delivered at a factory producing JCB construction equipment in the West Midlands on 28 November. His aim, he explained, would be to secure agreement on this as 'an absolute requirement'[29] in the re-negotiation that would precede the referendum he proposed to hold if he won the general election. To avoid falling foul of the EU's principle of freedom of movement, his ideas concentrated not on preventing immigrants from coming, but on making it less attractive for them to do so by limiting the benefits available to those who found work in this country. This was a clever idea. Its disadvantage was that it did not appease those in this country who wanted more immediate and extreme measures, while adding a big new element to his negotiating task and to the way in which the outcome of the negotiation would subsequently be judged by the British people.

To set against these setbacks and difficulties, Cameron could celebrate the decision of the Scottish people in the referendum held on 18 September 2014 to remain in the United Kingdom, an infinitely more important event than any by-election defeats. He had not himself been directly involved. The battle had been fought between Scots in Scotland, but the result could be claimed as a vindication of the agreement he had reached in 2013 with the Scottish first minister, Alex Salmond, to hold the referendum. It also encouraged him to believe that the success could be repeated in the referendum on Europe.

Cameron could take heart, too, from the performance of the economy, which, after years of austerity, was growing more rapidly than at any time since the pre-financial crisis year of 2006. The public sector deficit, to the reduction of which the government attached so much importance, had been halved and the rate of job creation was the best in Europe. In the polls he himself was well ahead of the new Labour leader, Ed Miliband.

Nonetheless, as May 2015 approached, few expected the Conservatives to win the general election outright. The universal expectation was for another hung Parliament. The bookmakers put the odds on this happening at 1/25. Cameron defied them handsomely by winning the first overall Conservative majority since Major's unexpected triumph in 1992. He did so as a result of two swings: from the Liberal Democrats to the Conservatives in England and from Labour to the SNP in Scotland. The final score was 330 Conservatives, 232 Labour, 8 Liberal Democrats, and 56 SNP.

UKIP had a bitter experience. In terms of votes cast, their 4 million, or 12.6 per cent of the total, put them well ahead of the Liberal Democrats' 2.4 million and 7.9 per cent. They came second in 120 seats yet managed to win only one. Their influence in the new Parliament was therefore nil, but in the country they represented a substantial body of opinion, with their support drawn mainly from the Conservatives, from whom they took 2.5 votes for every one they took from Labour. An ominous omen for the forthcoming referendum.

Britain's European partners were disconcerted as well as surprised by the election result. They had assumed that, whatever combination of parties might form a new coalition, a referendum would be unlikely to take place. A Labour/SNP partnership would not want one, and in another Conservative/Liberal Democrat combination the Liberal Democrats would withhold their assent. They were probably right about what would have happened if there had been another coalition of either stripe, though given the strength and continued growth of the UKIP vote, the demand for a referendum, after so many earlier referendum promises had been broken, might have proved too strong to resist.

The incoming government wanted the referendum to take place as soon as possible. The sooner it was out of the way, and hopefully won, the sooner the Europe issue could be put to rest and ministers freed to get on with their domestic priorities. It also seemed sensible, to both the British and the EU, to avoid letting the negotiations run on into 2017, when they would get entangled with the French and German elections due to be held in that year. So, Cameron aimed to complete the negotiations by the end of the year if possible, and in early 2016 at the latest, in order to hold the referendum in June of that coming year.

His negotiating requirements were spelt out in two chapters in the Conservative Party's election manifesto. One, headed 'Real change in our relationship with the European Union', included a list of proposals for improving the way the EU worked that would benefit all members and re-affirmed British support for the single market. It expressed opposition to ever-closer union, to joining the Euro, to participating in Eurozone bailouts, to a constant flow of power to Brussels, and to a European army, distant though that particular prospect was.

The other, headed 'Controlled immigration that benefits Britain', set out a proposal for reducing the number of immigrants from other EU countries by making it less attractive for them to come here. This would be achieved by imposing a transition period during which new arrivals would be denied access to a range of in-work and child benefits and to social housing. In addition, those who failed to find a job within six months would be obliged to leave. To those in Britain who wanted a system for controlling the flow of people coming into this country, this proposal seemed far too modest. To those in other EU countries, who believed that all citizens of the EU should be treated equally whatever their nationality, it seemed outrageous.

Reconciling those two positions was always going to be difficult. The extent of the difficulty in Britain was demonstrated on 2 February 2016 in a House of Commons exchange on a letter sent by the president of the European Council, Donald Tusk, to Cameron, setting out the EU's response to the British government's formal proposals. It would form the basis on which the final round of negotiations would take place. When the minister for Europe, David Lidington, gave it a warm welcome, the Conservative MP Steve Barker described him as 'polishing poo' while Cash called it a 'pint-sized package'.[30] The reaction of the anti-Europe Conservative-supporting newspapers was similarly scornful. 'Who do you think you are kidding Mr Cameron?' asked *The Sun*, adding that there would be 'No Control of Our Borders'.[31] The rest of the right-wing press, the Conservative Party's habitual supporters, kept up this tone, until Cameron went to Brussels for the final round of negotiations on 18 February.

Had the British people voted to stay in the EU at the referendum, the deal he brought back would have represented a watershed, as much for the EU as for Britain. On the outstanding question of the EU's ultimate destination of ever-closer union, a matter of concern in Britain from the very beginning, he secured formal recognition that Britain 'is not committed to further political integration into the European Union'. This was not only a highly symbolic change that would have brought joy to the heart of Thatcher had she been alive to see it. It would have had legal implications as well, by curbing the European Court of Justice's scope for referring to the spirit of the treaties in decisions affecting Britain. Over time, some of the other member states that had not been present at the creation of the EU in the 1950s might well have sought a similar exemption. Even if they didn't, the principle had been established that not everyone was committed to working towards the same ultimate destination.

At the time of Maastricht, there had been a widespread fear among Eurosceptics that, despite the opt-out from EMU secured by Major, Britain would be unable to avoid being dragged along in its wake. In 2016 Cameron secured explicit safeguards for those member states outside the Eurozone relating to non-discrimination, not having to participate in bailouts, and keeping their own banking supervision and macro-prudential regulation of financial services. This was a significant breakthrough that, added to the opt-out from ever-closer union, would have put Britain's membership onto a new footing. It was, however, highly technical stuff, never likely to attract the attention of most of the media or to cut through to public opinion.

Public attention was focused, almost to the exclusion of everything else, on the section in the deal devoted to immigration. On this, what Cameron had asked for had fallen far short of what those in Britain who felt most strongly on the subject, including the press, demanded. What he brought back was a watered-down version of his original bid. In the eyes of the media and many in his own party, that more than outweighed what he had achieved on the other issues and was to prove a source of great weakness in the forthcoming referendum. It has been argued that he could have achieved more on immigration if he had really thought he was in danger of losing the referendum and had confronted the other EU leaders with that prospect. In the light of how the referendum campaign played out, I think the gap between the most the EU could have given on this point and what Cameron needed to convince the British electorate that he had brought about real change in the terms of British membership was just too great.

An indication of how tough the referendum would be came while Cameron was still in Brussels. The press conference at which he explained and justified his deal was carried live on the 10 p.m. news bulletins in London. He concluded with the words 'That is why I will be campaigning with all my heart and soul to persuade the British people to remain in the reformed European Union that we have secured today.'[32] Immediately afterwards came the announcement that Michael Gove, his close friend and the secretary of state for justice, would be supporting the Leave campaign. In the following days, five other Cabinet ministers made the same choice, plus, most damagingly of all, Cameron's fellow Old Etonian, the charismatic Mayor of London, Boris Johnson.[33]

Conclusions

The In/Out referendum held on 23 June 2016 was the culmination of a long struggle. Calls for a referendum on some aspect of Britain's relationship with the EU are a constantly recurring theme throughout the second half of this book. Thatcher set the ball rolling in the Commons debate before the Maastricht conference in 1991, when she demanded that Major should undertake to hold one before committing Britain to joining the Euro. In the following years, the Conservative and Labour parties both promised to do that. Later promises were made to hold a referendum before signing up to the proposed European Constitution, the Lisbon Treaty, and further transfers of power to Brussels. Even the Liberal Democrats, the most consistently pro-EU party of all, committed itself to the principle of an In/Out referendum in its 2010 general election manifesto. But none was held.

I never argued in favour of holding a referendum at the time these calls were being made. However, as I have already indicated, I now believe that it would have been a good thing if one or more had been held. A referendum on a specific issue, such as the proposed constitution or the Lisbon Treaty, would have obliged pro-Europeans to confront the underlying sovereignty issues that had been too often glossed over since Macmillan and Heath had rejected Kilmuir's advice to be frank about them. It would, at the same time, have forced us to set out the arguments in favour of remaining in the EU in terms of Britain's economic interests, its influence in the world, its shared values with other Europeans, and the benefits to be gained from working closely with them across a whole range of activities. It would also, I believe, have eased the British people's sense of being carried inexorably forward on a one-way tide to greater integration over which they had no control.

Defeat would not necessarily have precipitated an existential crisis in the country's membership of the EU, any more than was the case with the rejection of various EU proposals in referendums in France, the Netherlands, Denmark, and Ireland. Rather, it would have enabled both Pros and Antis to gauge the evolving state of public opinion on Europe and to adjust their policies and the balance of their arguments accordingly. Such referendums would have constituted a significant innovation in terms of British constitutional practice, but no more so than the 1975 referendum on Europe and those on Scottish and Welsh devolution in 1979, changing the voting system for UK-wide general elections in 2011, and Scottish independence in 2014.

By the time Cameron became prime minister in 2010, the pressure on him to call a referendum on Europe was becoming intense. Fuelled by mounting public concern at the remorseless rise in immigration, UKIP was winning over Conservative supporters and influencing opinion within the party, including the choice of Conservative candidates to fight the 2015 election. He and other mainstream Conservatives could see the party being pushed steadily to the right on what had come to be called cultural issues as well as on Europe. Rebellions by Conservative MPs over Europe-related matters were also becoming endemic.

Whether he needed to have gone for broke by promising to hold an In/Out referendum rather than one on a specific issue relating to British membership is another matter. If there had been some current EU proposal on the table that would have triggered a referendum in other member states, Cameron might have been able to use that as an issue on which to hold one here. In the absence of any such proposal, it is, at the very least, understandable that he should have decided to try to bring about changes in the EU that would enable Britain to feel more comfortable within it, and then to put the result to the people. The point made by Andrew Mitchell in Chapter Eight about using a national referendum to resolve an internal party issue remained valid. But that issue, tearing the heart of the governing party and fuelling the rise of UKIP and anti-EU feeling in the country at large, was threatening to make the whole conduct of British policy within the EU unmanageable. To go for a referendum was, as Cameron very well knew, a gamble, but so was standing out against one. If immigration had fallen rather than continued to rise between the Bloomberg speech in January 2013 and the referendum in June 2016, the gamble might well have come off.

The details of the 2016 referendum and why it ended as it did have been analysed and pored over in numerous books and academic papers.[1] I will not provide another comprehensive survey of the campaign here. My story is the Conservative Party and Europe. I will, therefore, confine myself to discussing the party's crucial role in determining the outcome of the referendum. The margin of victory in favour of Britain leaving the EU was close – 51.9 per cent to 48.1. In such a situation, any one of a host of factors can be said to have made the difference between defeat and victory. In this case, none counted for more than the decision of 61 per cent of those who had voted Conservative in the 2015 general election to vote Leave in the referendum. It illustrates how much of the Conservative base had been won over by UKIP's arguments and the cost of the failure by Cameron and his colleagues since 2005 ever to make the case for staying in.

By comparison, 65 per cent of those who had voted Labour and 68 per cent of those who had voted Liberal Democrat cast their ballots for Remain. Which poses an interesting question.

With the result so finely balanced, might not a Labour leader more enthusiastic for Remain than Jeremy Corbyn have swung it the other way?

It was not only Conservative votes that won the battle for Leave. It was Conservative leadership as well. The referendum was, in effect, a Conservative civil war, with the party providing the leading protagonists for both sides – Cameron and Osborne for Remain and Johnson and Gove for Leave. It was on them rather than on the activities of the official cross-party organisations, Britain Stronger in Europe and Vote Leave, that the public focused.

If it had not been for Johnson and Gove, the face of the Leave campaign would probably have been Farage, a formidable campaigner, but, like Enoch Powell and Tony Benn on the Leave side in 1975, a deeply divisive figure. He could rouse a 'People's Army' and he, more than any other single individual, had created the conditions that forced Cameron to call the referendum, but only credible heavyweight Conservative politicians could have persuaded such a large majority of those who had voted Conservative in 2015, including many swing voters, to go against the prime minister in 2016. In the view of Matthew Elliott, the chief executive of the Vote Leave Campaign, 'Boris Johnson did more than anybody to give swing voters the confidence to vote Leave.'[2] The hearts of those who did so would always have inclined them towards Leave, but, without the intervention of Johnson and Gove, the heads and the votes of many of them would have been put off by Farage and swayed by the prestige of Cameron's office and the authority it gave to his arguments.

Not only that: if Farage, or someone else from another party, had been leading the Leave campaign, Cameron would have felt no inhibitions about attacking them. He held back from doing so against Johnson, Gove, and the other Conservative ministers and MPs on the Leave side because his eyes were set on leading a united government and party after having won the referendum.

They felt under no such constraint, and the ferocity of their attacks was a source of resentment among his entourage.[3]

The presence of serious Conservative politicians on the Leave side increased its capacity to raise large sums of money. With Dominic Cummings as its campaign director, Vote Leave was in any case by some margin the more effective of the two cross-party groups. Lavish financial resources provided him with the means to deploy his skills to their fullest extent.

Within the Conservative Party, those campaigning for Leave had the inestimable advantage of being in line with the tide of Conservative opinion over the previous twenty-eight years, as I have shown in the preceding chapters. Ever since Margaret Thatcher's Bruges speech in 1988 and her fall from power two years later, opinion in the party had been moving against Europe. From the end of the Major government in 1997, increasing numbers of MPs and core voters had become ever more open to the arguments of those who wanted to take Britain out of the EU. Since that time, those in favour of closer involvement with the EU and making the case for Britain to be an active member had been fighting a rearguard action.

By 2016 the great majority of party members were deeply sceptical about Europe. Against that background, Cameron did well not to lose more of his senior ministers than the five who followed Gove. They were the former party leader Iain Duncan Smith, Chris Grayling, Theresa Villiers, Priti Patel, and John Whittingdale. Osborne had to work hard to keep Sajid Javid on board, as did Cameron with Liz Truss. The home secretary, Theresa May, took some time to declare for Remain and was then distinctly cautious about venturing onto the campaign trail. A majority of MPs came out for Remain, but some of the Remainers were more in the nature of camp followers than campaigners, as they took care not to create trouble with their Leave-supporting constituency associations.

An example of what an MP with strong convictions could, over time, achieve in terms of influencing his constituents is provided by Clarke, who had been MP for Rushcliffe since 1970. Although situated in the strongly pro-Leave East Midlands, it voted 58 per cent to 42 for Remain. No other MP had the same combination of stature, longevity, and devotion both to his constituency and to the European cause as Clarke, so it is impossible to generalise from this example. It does, however, show how influential over time an individual MP's example could be.

The Conservative-supporting newspapers were never going to support Cameron. They had been hostile to the EU for many decades and had rubbished his negotiating tactics in Brussels as well as the deal he brought back. Throughout the campaign, all the papers that carried most weight with the Conservative rank and file – the two *Telegraph* titles, the *Daily Mail*, *The Sun*, and the *Daily Express* – were vociferous supporters of Leave. This deprived Cameron of one of his normal means of communicating with his support base and was bound to call his position at the head of his party into question. In their monumental volume *Cameron at 10: The Verdict*, Anthony Seldon and Peter Snowdon allege that bringing about a change of leader was in fact the intention of Rupert Murdoch and Paul Dacre, the editor of the *Daily Mail*.[4]

As the referendum campaign proceeded, the Conservatives on both sides made wild and unsustainable claims. Among the most notorious on the Leave side was the one emblazoned on Johnson's and Gove's battle bus that £350 million a week was going from Britain to the EU and could be re-allocated to the NHS after leaving the EU. On the Remain side, it was the draft emergency budget, raising income tax and cutting spending on the NHS and other public services, that Osborne claimed he would have to introduce if the country voted to Leave. All election campaigns play fast and loose with facts and figures. Few in British political history have rivalled the 2016 referendum in that respect.

The ace in the Leavers' pack of cards was immigration. It became even more advantageous to them during the course of the campaign when, in May, the Office of National Statistics announced that in 2015 the net rate had reached 330,000. The contrast between this figure and Cameron's promise of a reduction to the tens of thousands was devastating to his credibility, as the right-wing press and the Leave campaigners plugged away ceaselessly at his 'broken promise'. During the six weeks running up to polling day, Cameron himself recorded that the *Daily Mail* 'ran eighteen immigration-related front page stories'.[5]

When the campaign began, the Remainers believed they could trump immigration with economic arguments. As Cameron's director of communications, Craig Oliver, has explained, 'Our campaign was based on the simple proposition that electorates don't vote against their own pockets ... The view that the economy would trump immigration as the primary concern of voters was backed up by plenty of solid polling evidence as well as the pattern of how electorates had behaved going back over a century. It was wrong – and devastatingly so when we did not have enough of an answer on freedom of movement.'[6] Vernon Bogdanor has made the same point when comparing the 1975 and 2016 referendums:

In 2016 the fear element, which had worked in favour of remaining in 1975, now worked in favour of leaving. There was a greater fear of being dragged into integrationist projects and, above all, a greater fear of uncontrolled immigration than fear of the economic consequences of Brexit.[7]

This was not the only problem with the economic argument. In 1975, the prominent economists and leaders of business and industry who argued that leaving would damage the economy and thus be bad for employment and wages had carried considerable weight. In 2016, that was not the case. The authority of economists had been badly damaged by the 2008 financial crash, which they had failed to foresee, and by its consequences. The leaders of business and industry, with their stratospheric remuneration, were regarded as the beneficiaries and apostles of the very globalisation and technological change that were disrupting the lives of those who worked in traditional industries. Bankers and those speaking for the City of London were particularly abhorred. The views of authoritative international and foreign-based bodies, including the International Monetary Fund, the World Trade Organization, and the US Federal Reserve, all of which said the British economy would be damaged by leaving the EU, were similarly distrusted for the same reason. When Gove told a Sky News question-and-answer audience that 'people in this country have had enough of experts',[8] he encapsulated the resentment of the many suffering from, and fearful of, change against those they felt were benefitting from it.

The economic argument was further handicapped by the record in government of the two most prominent politicians who were making it. After becoming prime minister and chancellor of the exchequer, respectively, in 2010, Cameron and Osborne had pursued an economic policy of rigid austerity aimed at reducing the public sector deficit. This had led to a prolonged squeeze on the resources available for health, education, and welfare. Those who had borne the brunt of this policy – the less well-off and the regions suffering from the greatest economic difficulties – felt correspondingly resentful. Together they constituted a sizeable bloc of people who felt neglected by government, at the mercy of external forces beyond their control, and cut off from any prospect of material improvement.

That had not prevented the Conservatives from winning the

2015 general election. Widespread lack of confidence in Labour's economic competence, fear that a Labour government would be in hock to the SNP, and the perceived inadequacies of the then Labour leader, Ed Miliband, had proved to be more potent factors. Coming as it did a year later, the referendum provided an opportunity for all who felt aggrieved, however they had voted at the election, to strike a blow at those they held responsible for their difficulties. Vote Leave skilfully and unscrupulously presented the EU as epitomising the external forces that were making their lives more difficult, which gave them an additional reason for doing so.

In addition to all the above, and as I have already pointed out, Cameron's own record as a Eurosceptic rendered him an unconvincing advocate of Britain remaining in the EU. He recognises this in his memoirs when he writes, 'Our enthusiasm for the Remain case could easily be questioned. After all, we had shifted very quickly from "big, bossy and interfering" negativity to "stronger, safer and better off" positivity. We were asking a lot of people to believe such a handbrake turn.'[9]

It was indeed asking a lot and, not surprisingly, his sudden change of direction was met with a good deal of cynicism. He admits that he should have done more 'to mix criticisms of the EU with talking about its very real achievements; not least two longstanding British objectives of creating the single market and enlarging the EU to take in countries that had emerged from decades of state socialism'.[10] He also sought to remind people of the sacrifices Britain had made on behalf of freedom in Europe in the two world wars by evoking 'the serried rows of white headstones in lovingly-tended Commonwealth war cemeteries [that] stand as silent testament to the price this country has paid to help restore peace and order in Europe'.[11] But, by then, it was too late. If he had been speaking up for the EU and Britain's role within it over the years, instead of constantly grumbling about it and criticising, he would have carried greater conviction.

There was never any doubt about Cameron's commitment to winning nor about the effort he put into doing so. He campaigned hard and effectively. He was invariably eloquent and the master of his brief when arguing the case for Remain in speeches and question-and-answer sessions. But more than effort and eloquence were required to carry the day. He needed a degree of passion and vision that did not lie within him. In 1975, Jenkins and Heath had had that vision and passion. They had been able to invoke the big issues of war and peace, while basing their case for staying in on economic self-interest. In 2016, Cameron and Osborne could not match them in appropriately contemporary terms.

What if Remain had nonetheless won? For Cameron it would have been a huge personal success. He would have been responsible for submitting two important constitutional decisions to a referendum – Scottish independence being the other one – and getting the result he wanted in both. He had led Britain's only coalition government since the war and he had won the 2015 general election. With that record, he would have been hailed as a political mastermind. During the 2016 referendum campaign, there had been some talk on the Leave side of mounting a leadership challenge after a Remain victory, as the result would have thwarted the wishes of the great majority of party members.

I cannot believe it would have succeeded. Cameron would have taken great pains to bring the party together by mollifying the membership and ensuring that his Cabinet was balanced between winners and losers. He had a programme of domestic legislation ready to go and was already pledged to retire before the next election. If there was to be a reckoning between winners and losers, it would have been in the interests of everyone to leave it until his departure. At that point, either Johnson or Gove, or perhaps both, could have challenged Osborne for the crown.

In the EU, Cameron would have earned enormous credit. His fellow heads of state and government in the European Council would all have remembered how in referendums in France and the Netherlands, two of the six founding members, the people had rejected the proposal for a European Constitution. In 1992, the French referendum on whether to join the Euro had been won by only the narrowest of margins. Other European proposals had at different times been defeated in Ireland and Denmark. Few of them could have felt confident that if they had to put another EU proposition to their people, it would be carried. They would have admired Cameron's victory and given him credit for pulling it off.

British circumstances were unique. In no other EU country was there any significant body of opinion that over the years had been seeking to call membership of the EU into question. No other government would have dreamt for one moment of asking the question of their people that Cameron asked. If they had, who knows what might have had happened. When, in January 2018, the BBC's Andrew Marr asked President Macron whether, if the French had been asked the same question as the British, they would have voted the same way, he conceded that they might.[12]

To speculate on what might have happened in the Conservative Party, in Britain more widely, and to the cause of Britain in Europe after the plaudits had died away, is an unprofitable exercise. Hostility to the EU had become so deeply embedded in the party and the country that it would no more have been extinguished by the referendum result than was the movement for Scottish independence by the Scottish referendum of 2014. The issues of sovereignty and national identity that lay at the heart of that hostility would not have died away. A segment of the population would have continued to worry about them, but they would not have been most people's primary political concerns.

If immigration had remained a big issue, anti-EU feeling would have continued to complicate Britain's relationship with its partners. Cameron might even have found himself forced to re-open that aspect of the negotiation. If large-scale immigration from the rest of Europe had dropped down the political agenda, the public's interest in the Leave case would probably have likewise diminished.

Even so, the embers of anti-Europeanism would have remained. If not Farage, then somebody else would, no doubt, sooner or later have sought to re-ignite them. That would, I think, have been more difficult than in the past. By removing the commitment to ever-closer union and by ring-fencing Britain from the Eurozone, Cameron's deal would have put British membership of the EU onto an entirely new footing: one that might have set a precedent for some other member states that had not been among the six founder members. Whether or not that happened, it would have provided the basis for Britain to build a more harmonious and constructive relationship with its partners than had existed before. The British people would have given their verdict. They would also have had a clearer idea of what they had signed up to than at any time since Macmillan and Heath had disregarded Kilmuir's advice to be frank about the sovereignty implications of membership.

When future generations look back on this period in our national history, they are, I think, unlikely to be surprised by the result of the referendum. The deep grumbling discontent with membership that had for so long characterised the British relationship with the EU – the worm in the apple referred to in the Introduction to this book – will account for that. What will, I think, surprise them is that Britain should have taken so momentous a step as to leave the EU, after over forty years of membership, with so little preparation.

Those advocating Leave had no plan for how to make the

break. They presented no assessments about what it would mean for the British economy and for British trade. They had nothing to say about the implications of leaving the EU for Britain's wider international relationships. They failed to take account of the consequences for Northern Ireland, a domestic UK issue of the utmost sensitivity. They had argued for a referendum for decades. They had looked forward to it resulting in a vote to leave. But they had no clear idea about how to proceed if the great day should ever arrive and no plans for how to face the future. There was something incredibly casual about the whole enterprise. It was as if they never believed in their heart of hearts that the opportunity to leave the EU would ever arise and were taken by surprise when it did.

Cameron stood down after losing the referendum, and Theresa May was elected to succeed him. She became notorious for intoning 'Brexit means Brexit'. In fact, neither she nor anybody else had a clear idea of what it meant or how to achieve it. Did the country wish to remain as close as possible to the EU or to distance itself as far as it could? In other words, a soft or a hard Brexit? Did it wish to prioritise access to the single market for its goods and services or was it willing to sacrifice that advantage to recover more freedom of action to run its own affairs? How was the commitment not to create a land border between Northern Ireland and the Republic of Ireland to be reconciled with the establishment of border controls between the UK and the EU? Because none of these issues was properly thrashed out within the government before the withdrawal negotiations began, the British negotiators were at a permanent disadvantage in their dealings with the Commission representing the EU. Four years were required between the referendum in June 2016 and the end of the transition period on 31 December 2020 to reach agreement on the terms of the departure and the new relationship. Even then, a host of practical issues remained unresolved, with those relating to Northern Ireland and fishing rights the most troublesome.

During those four years, the Conservative Party won two general elections against the backdrop of a struggle for power within its own ranks. May called the first in June 2017 to secure a mandate of her own, and to consolidate her authority over her MPs and the negotiations with the EU. Her gamble failed. When the party lost both seats and its overall majority in the House of Commons, her authority was fatally weakened.[13] She could no longer rely on the loyalty of ministers or backbenchers nor preside over a coherent negotiation with the EU. In July 2019, after two chaotic years, she resigned and was succeeded by Johnson at the head of a government committed to the most complete, or hardest, form of break with the EU. Those MPs, among them friends of mine, who opposed this in favour of a softer Brexit were either ejected from the party or banished to the sidelines. When, in December 2019, Johnson won a substantial majority in a hastily called general election, the victory of those within the Conservative Party whose views were closest to UKIP was complete.

Complete does not necessarily mean enduring. History shows that a party that has become habituated to civil war cannot easily set aside the practice. The settlement of the issue that provoked it may simply mean that the infighting breaks out again on other matters. That was the Conservative experience during 2021. Against the background of the Covid pandemic, party discipline broke down and backbench rebellions became endemic. Issues of probity and personal behaviour also arose around the prime minister to further diminish his authority. As I sign off this book in early December 2021, the upheavals look set to continue.

The problems left unresolved between Britain and the EU at the end of the transition period meant that in January 2021, the relationship between the two sides got off to a disputatious start. The undisguised desire of some on the EU side for Britain to be seen to be paying a price for leaving made it more difficult, as did the aggressiveness with which the British government approached some of the outstanding problems. Covid added further complications. Some years may well be required before the relationship reaches an equilibrium, as the two sides work through the challenges inherent in the new situation.

For Britain, the principal challenge is to be next door to a much larger and more powerful neighbour that is also its principal trading partner: a situation akin to Canada's and Mexico's vis-à-vis the United States. There may be times when that could become very uncomfortable. As those two countries know from experience, the larger partner may, at any time, be tempted to bully its smaller neighbours in pursuit of what it perceives to be its own interests, or to adopt policies without regard to how its neighbours might be affected. On this side of the Atlantic, further problems could stem from the EU's practice of trying, whenever possible, to use its negotiating strength to limit the freedom of manoeuvre of its smaller neighbours.

For the EU, the principal challenge is to have a neighbour of sufficient scale to be able to pursue independent policies, which, if successful, will provide a template against which the people of the member states will judge its own performance. This is a not inconsiderable threat for an organisation that depends for its legitimacy above all on the benefits it can deliver to its citizens, and is engaged in a perpetual struggle to keep its member states in line. The resentment displayed by the Commission and some member states at Britain's greater success with the roll-out of the anti-coronavirus vaccine in the first half of 2021 shows how unwelcome that challenge is. Given the cumbersome nature of EU decision-making, other such situations may arise in the future. Another potential source of discontent within the EU could develop if the citizens of some member states should at any time feel that Eurozone policies are holding back their economies compared with Britain.

The worm that ate away at the legitimacy of Britain's membership of the EU and the pain of the divorce negotiations have made it impossible to restore the status quo ante. There can be no going back. A new relationship must be created. In the light of history, geography, trading links, common security concerns, and personal relationships, it would be better for both sides if it were as amicable and constructive as possible.

I hope that this account, fifty years after Britain decided to join what became the EU, of how and why, to my great regret, the Conservative Party turned against Europe will contribute to bringing that about. I further hope that, now that Britain is on its own, the Conservative Party will contribute to the creation of a new, close, harmonious, and mutually advantageous relationship with the EU and its member states.

Notes

Introduction
1. Christopher Tugendhat, *Making Sense of Europe* (Viking, 1986).

1. Missed Opportunities 1946–1959
1. Until 1990, Germany was divided into West Germany and East Germany.
2. I will use the acronym EEC until 1993 and then EU. In the early years, the institution was often called the Common Market, and during the period in question I will refer to it by that name as well.
3. Jean Monnet, *Memoirs* transl. Richard Mayne (Collins, 1997) p. 281.
4. Winston Churchill, speech delivered at the University of Zurich, 19 September 1946.
5. Martin Gilbert, *Winston Churchill* Volume VII *Never Despair, 1945–1965* (Heinemann, 1988) pp. 286–7.
6. Peter Hennessy, *Having It So Good* (Penguin, 2007) p. 320.
7. 1951 Conservative Party general election manifesto.
8. Roy Jenkins, *Churchill* (Macmillan, 2001) p. 817.
9. *Ibid.* pp. 817–18
10. Winston Churchill, speech delivered at the University of Zurich, 19 September 1946.

11. Winston Churchill addressing the Congress of Europe at The Hague, 7 May 1948.
12. Monnet p. 312.
13. Dean Acheson, *Present at the Creation* (Hamish Hamilton, 1970) p. 385.
14. *Ibid.* p. 386.
15. Hansard, HC vol 476, cols 1963–4 (26 June 1950).
16. Sandra D. Onslow, 'Backbench Debate within the Conservative Party and its influence on British Foreign Policy, 1948–57', PhD thesis, London School of Economics, (UMI Dissertation Publishing), 1994.
17. Alistair Horne, *Macmillan 1894–1956* (Pan Macmillan, 1988) p. 351.
18. Monnet p. 316.
19. *Ibid.*
20. Hugo Young, *This Blessed Plot* (Macmillan, 1998) p. 73.
21. Hennessy p. 292.
22. *Ibid.* p. 293.
23. Harold Macmillan, *Riding The Storm 1956–59* (Macmillan, 1971) pp. 77–8.
24. Young p. 80.
25. Young p. 83.
26. He subsequently resigned from the government in protest against the Suez invasion.
27. Hennessy p. 398.
28. Robert Marjolin, *Architect of European Unity* transl. William Hall (Weidenfeld and Nicolson, 1989) p. 333.
29. Macmillan p. 85.
30. N. J. Crowson, The *Conservative Party and European Integration since 1945* (Routledge, 2007) p. 26.
31. Young p. 109
32. Now Lord Jopling.
33. Private conversation with Lord Jopling, 18 May 2020.

2. Macmillan's False Start 1959–1963

1. Harold Macmillan, *At the End of the Day 1961–63* (Macmillan, 1973) p. 1.
2. *Ibid*. p. 1.
3. Alistair Horne, *Macmillan 1957–1986* (Macmillan, 1989) p. 231.
4. Quoted in *Ibid*. p. 256.
5. *Ibid*. p. 246.
6. Lady Dorothy Macmillan's father was the ninth Duke of Devonshire.
7. Horne p. 253.
8. Peter Hennessy, *Winds of Change* (Allen Lane, 2019) p. 73.
9. Kilmuir and Macmillan had a misfortune in common. As was well known in political circles, both of their wives had long-running affairs with other men; in Lady Dorothy's case with another MP, Bob Boothby, who Macmillan very generously made a life peer in 1958; in Lady Kilmuir's with Lord De la Warr.
10. Hugo Young, *This Blessed Plot* (Macmillan, 1998) p. 126.
11. Hennessy p. 75.
12. Hansard, HC vol 645, col 1481 (2 August 1961).
13. Macmillan p. 352.
14. Hennessy p. 96.
15. Young p. 140.
16. Macmillan p. 26.
17. Margaret Thatcher, *The Path to Power* (HarperCollins, 1995) p. 127.
18. Robert Shepherd, *Enoch Powell: A Biography* (Hutchinson, 1996) p. 248.
19. Hennessy p. 160.
20. One of his successes was an impersonation of Macmillan speaking in French about Le Marche Commun at a white-tie dinner at Versailles hosted by de Gaulle. Private

Conversation with Lord Lang of Monkton, 18 November 2020.

21. Nigel Fisher, *Iain MacLeod* (Andre Deutsch, 1973) p. 222.
22. Janet Morgan (ed.), *The Backbench Diaries of Richard Crossman* (Hamish Hamilton and Jonathan Cape 1981) p. 964.
23. Hugh Gaitskell, speech to the Labour Party conference, Brighton, 3 October 1962.
24. Macmillan p. 129.
25. Edward Heath, *The Course of My Life: The Autobiography* (Hodder & Stoughton, 1998) p. 213.
26. *Ibid.*
27. *The Economist* (13 June 2009)
28. Robert Marjolin, *Architect of European Unity* transl. William Hall (Weidenfeld and Nicolson, 1989) p. 313.
29. *Ibid.* p. 338.
30. Macmillan p. 365.
31. Heath p. 240.

3. Heath's Triumph and Tragedy 1963–1975

1. Private conversation with Lord Jopling.
2. Philip Ziegler, *Edward Heath: The Authorised Biography* (Harper Press, 2010) p. 159.
3. *Putting Britain Right Ahead: A statement of Conservative Aims* (Conservative Central Office, 1965).
4. The sibyls were female prophets or oracles in the ancient world. Powell was a classical scholar who, in 1937, at the age of twenty-five, had been appointed Professor of Greek at the University of Sydney.
5. Speech at a meeting of the Conservative Political Centre, Birmingham, 20 April 1968.
6. Now Lord Howell of Guildford and Lord Marlesford.
7. Private conversation with Lord Howell, 7 June 2020.

8. Richard Crossman, *The Diaries of a Cabinet Minister* Volume 1 *Minister of Housing* (Hamish Hamilton and Jonathan Cape, 1975) p. 461.

9. Hugo Young, *This Blessed Plot* (Macmillan, 1998) p. 197.

10. 'Now Britain's Strong – Let's Make it Great to Live In', Labour Party general election manifesto, 1970.

11. 'A Better Tomorrow', Conservative Party general election manifesto, 1970.

12. Tony Benn, *Office Without Power Diaries 1968–72* (Hutchinson, 1988) p. 293.

13. Private conversation with Sara Morrison, 6 July 2020.

14. Douglas Hurd, *An End to Promises* (Collins, 1979) p. 22.

15. Heath p. 307.

16. Hurd p. 26.

17. Nigel Fisher, *Iain MacLeod* (Andre Deutsch, 1973) p. 322.

18. Speech to the British Chamber of Commerce in Paris, 6 May 1970.

19. Hurd p. 60.

20. Ziegler p. 195.

21. N. J. Crowson, *The Conservative Party and European Integration since 1945: At the Heart of Europe* (Routledge, 2007) p. 36.

22. Young p. 228, quoting from *Report on the Negotiations for Entry into the European Community June 1970–July 1972*. At the time Young was writing, this report had not been published. In 2000, it was published under the title *Britain's Entry into the European Community: Report by Sir Con O'Neill on the Negotiations of 1970–1972*, edited by Sir David Hannay, now Lord Hannay of Chiswick.

23. *Ibid.*

24. *Ibid.* p. 226.

25. Hurd p. 64.

26. Simon Heffer, *Like the Roman: The Life of Enoch Powell* (Weidenfeld & Nicolson, 1998) p. 604.
27. Ziegler p. 286.
28. In strictly legal terms, there were still three communities: the original ECSC; Euratom, which dealt with atomic energy; and the EEC. In practice they functioned as one, with the same Council of Ministers and only one Commission.
29. Private conversation with Sara Morrison, 6 July 2020.
30. Geoffrey Howe, *Conflict of Loyalty* (Macmillan, 1995) p. 68.
31. Heffer p. 620.
32. Private conversation with Lord Jopling, 7 July 2020.
33. Heffer p. 640.
34. Hansard, HC vol 823, cols 912–1071 (21 October 1971).
35. *Ibid.*
36. Private conversation with Lord Lamont, 5 August 2020.
37. Speech at the West Point Military Academy, 5 December 1962.
38. Ziegler p. 295.

4. The 1975 Referendum – Before and After

1. Cecil King, *The Cecil King Diary 1970–1974* (Jonathan Cape, 1975) pp. 349, 367, 376, 387.
2. Michael Heseltine, *Life in the Jungle: My Autobiography* (Hodder & Stoughton, 2001) p. 161.
3. Barbara Castle, *The Castle Diaries 1974–76* (Weidenfeld and Nicolson, 1980) p. 311.
4. Mark Garnett and Ian Aitken, *Splendid! Splendid! The Authorised Biography of Willie Whitelaw* (Jonathan Cape, 2002) p. 215.
5. John Biffen, *Semi-Detached* (Biteback Publishing, 2013) p. 267.

6. Charles Moore, *Margaret Thatcher: The Authorised Biography* Volume I *Not For Turning* (Allen Lane, 2014) p. 299.

7. Bernard Donoughue, *Downing Street Diary: With Harold Wilson in No 10* (Jonathan Cape, 2004) p. 257.

8. Hugo Young, *This Blessed Plot* (Macmillan, 1998) p. 281.

9. Speech to London University Students' Association, 7 March 1975.

10. Philip Ziegler, *Edward Heath: The Authorised Biography* (Harper Press, 2010) p. 496.

11. Castle p. 406.

12. William Whitelaw, *The Whitelaw Memoirs* (Aurum Press, 1989) p. 145.

13. Roy Jenkins, *A Life at the Centre* (Macmillan, 1991) p. 416.

14. Castle p. 391.

15. 'The Choice Before Us', *Daily Telegraph* (4 June 1975).

16. This phrase was frequently attributed to him at the time and has been since in books and articles about the referendum, but I have never been able to establish its origin.

17. Young p. 293.

18. *Why You Should Vote No* (Her Majesty's Stationery Office, 1975).

19. Robert Saunders, *Yes to Europe: The 1975 Referendum and Seventies Britain* (Cambridge University Press, 2018) p. 84.

20. *Ibid.* p. 84.

21. *Ibid.* p. 373.

22. Jenkins p. 425.

23. 'Wet' was a derogatory term used by allies of Margaret Thatcher in Parliament and the media to describe those on the left of the party, whether in government, like Jim Prior and Sir Ian Gilmour, on the backbenches, or outside Parliament. I would have been regarded as a Wet.

24. Jenkins p. 426.
25. Caroline Jackson, 'The First British MEPs', *Journal of Contemporary History*, 2/2 (1993).
26. The appointment of commissioners at that time was made by the EEC Council of Ministers, which always accepted the names proposed by the governments of the member states. These names were then put to the Parliament, which voted to accept or reject them en bloc. In practice it always accepted them, until, in 1994, a hearings procedure was introduced. It then became necessary for each nominee to be approved by a Parliamentary committee before the Parliament voted on the incoming team as a whole.

5. Thatcher's Battles 1979–1991

1. Private conversation with Lord Powell of Bayswater, 9 September 2020.
2. Charles Powell, 'Margaret Thatcher' in Andrew Adonis (ed.), *Half In Half Out* (Biteback Publishing, 2018) p. 150.
3. Private conversation with Lord Howell of Guildford, 12 May 2020.
4. The fact that an issue is insignificant in GDP terms can be a misleading guide to its political importance. During the post-Brexit negotiations between Britain and the EU over a new trading relationship, one of the most intractable issues was fish, which accounted for less than 0.1 per cent of the economies of the two sides.
5. Margaret Thatcher, *The Downing Street Years* (HarperCollins, 1993) p. 79.
6. Sara Morrison recalls taking charge of the arrangements when, on more than one occasion, the president came to dinner at Heath's house in Wilton Street. Private conversation, 6 May 2020.

7. Alan Clark (ed.), *Diaries: Into Politics* (Weidenfeld and Nicolson, 2000) p. 139.

8. John Newhouse, 'The Diplomatic Round', *New Yorker* (22 October 1984).

9. He is said to have described Margaret Thatcher as having the eyes of Caligula and the lips of Marilyn Monroe, though not even Charles Powell can trace the origin of this story.

10. Francis Pym, *The Politics of Consent* (Hamish Hamilton, 1984) p. 74.

11. Thatcher p. 727.

12. Anthony Forster, *Euroscepticism in Contemporary British Politics Opposition in the British Conservative and Labour Parties since 1945* (Routledge, 2002) p. 69.

13. Thatcher p. 81.

14. When I went to take my formal leave of Margaret Thatcher before standing down, she gave me tea in her room in the House of Commons. She enquired warmly about my family, where we were going to live, and where our children would go to school. She was very interested in the mechanics of moving house. She then told me that she would do nothing to stand in my way if I wished to try to return to the House of Commons, but that if I succeeded, I could not expect to join her government, at least for a long time ahead. I had, however, already decided not to do so, and maintained that position even after receiving an approach from the officers of a strongly pro-EU constituency association in a safe Conservative seat.

15. Geoffrey Howe, *Conflict of Loyalty* (Macmillan, 1994) p. 405.

16. The system was not 'one country, one vote'. It was qualified by weightings broadly reflecting population that gave larger countries more voting power than smaller ones.

17. John Biffen, *Semi-Detached* (Biteback Publishing, 2013) p. 393.
18. Norman Fowler, *A Political Suicide* (Politico's, 2008) p. 49.
19. Her dislike of the Germans was something of a fixation. Some years after her fall, we were together at a party in a flat overlooking the Houses of Parliament. As we looked out of the window, she turned to me and said, 'Your Germans tried to destroy that, Christopher. Don't ever forget it.'
20. Speech to the European Parliament, 6 July 1988.
21. Speech to the College of Europe, 20 September 1988.
22. *Ibid.*
23. *Ibid.*
24. Speech to the Conservative Party conference at Brighton, 14 October 1988.
25. *Ibid.*
26. Christopher Tugendhat, *Making Sense of Europe* (Viking, 1986).
27. Howe p. 538.
28. Michael Heseltine, *Life in the Jungle My Autobiography* (Hodder & Stoughton, 2000) p. 348.
29. Private conversation with Anthony Teasdale, Howe's Special Adviser 1998–2000, 26 October 2020.
30. According to a (no doubt apocryphal) story that circulated at the time, Mitterrand said to Kohl, 'You can have the other half of Germany, if I can have half the Deutsche Mark.'
31. Fowler p. 51.
32. John Major, *John Major: The Autobiography* (HarperCollins, 1999) p. 168.
33. Meyer's constituency association in Clwyd North West did not approve of his challenge and in January 1990 de-selected him as their candidate at the next election.

34. The circumstances of this by-election were particularly poignant for Margaret Thatcher. It was held because of the murder by the IRA of the sitting MP, Ian Gow, who had been her devoted parliamentary private secretary from 1979 to 1983. Her period as leader of the Conservative Party was thus bookended by IRA murders of men who had been close to her: Airey Neave at the outset and Ian Gow at the close. She herself narrowly escaped death when the IRA blew up the Grand Hotel, Brighton, while she was staying there during the 1984 Conservative Party conference.
35. Private conversation with Lord Baker of Dorking, 16 March 2021.
36. *Prospect* (December 2020).
37. Max Hastings, *Editor* (Macmillan, 2002) p. 187.

6. Things Fall Apart 1991–1997

1. Private conversation with Lord Baker of Dorking, 16 March 2021.
2. John Major, *John Major: The Autobiography* (HarperCollins, 1999) p. 202.
3. *Ibid*. p. 202.
4. Now Lord Fowler.
5. Norman Fowler, *A Political Suicide* (Politico's, 2008) p. 303.
6. Private correspondence with David Nicholson.
7. Michael Spicer, *The Spicer Diaries* (Biteback Publishing, 2012) p. 180.
8. Still the capital of the then newly united Germany before it moved to Berlin.
9. Sarah Hogg and Jonathan Hill, *Too Close to Call: Power and Politics – John Major in No 10* (Little, Brown and Company, 1995) p. 79.
10. Fowler p. 84.
11. Spicer p. 193.

12. Major p. 288.
13. Hogg and Hill p.160.
14. Dominic Lawson, 'Saying the unsayable about the Germans', *The Spectator* (14 July 1990).
15. Charles Moore, *Margaret Thatcher: The Authorised Biography* Volume III *Herself Alone* (Allen Lane, 2019) p. 552.
16. William Cash, *Against a Federal Europe: The Battle for Britain* (Duckworth, 1991) p. 83.
17. Now Lord Patten of Barnes.
18. Private conversation with Lord Patten of Barnes, 16 November 2020.
19. Now Lord Radice.
20. Giles Radice, *Diaries 1980–2001: From Political Disaster to Election Triumph* (Weidenfeld & Nicolson, 2004) p. 270.
21. Margaret Thatcher, 'Don't Undo My Work', *Newsweek* (27 April 1992).
22. Spicer pp. 205–6.
23. Now Lord Ryder of Wensum.
24. Major p. 348.
25. Now Lord Clarke of Nottingham.
26. Fowler p. 133.
27. Now Lord Robertson of Port Ellen.
28. Major p. 348.
29. Spicer p. 213.
30. Radice p. 286.
31. Major pp. 367–8.
32. Theresa Gorman with Heather Kirby, *The Bastards – Dirty Tricks and the Challenge to Europe* (Macmillan, 1993).
33. Thatcher Vol. III. p. 803.
34. Private conversation with Lord Lamont of Lerwick, 26 November 2020.
35. Speech to the Selsdon Group, 11 October 1994.

36. *The Times* (12 October 1994).

37. Vernon Bogdanor, *Britain & Europe in a Troubled World* (Yale University Press, 2020) p. 94.

38. Now Lord Black of Crossharbour.

7. Three Leaders 1997–2005

1. Hansard, HC vol 294, col 68 (14 May 1997).

2. Tim Bale, *The Conservative Party from Thatcher to Cameron*, 2nd edition (Polity Press, 2016) p. 59.

3. Hansard, HL vol 808, col 1900 (30 December 2020).

4. Michael Spicer, *The Spicer Diaries* (Biteback Publishing, 2012) p. 326.

5. John Major, *John Major: The Autobiography* (HarperCollins, 1999) p. 202.

6. *The Economist* (19 May 1997).

7. Ken Clarke, *Kind of Blue: A Political Memoir* (Pan Books, 2017) p. 400.

8. Roy Jenkins, with whom I had remained on close terms since returning from Brussels, tried to argue me out of my position, but neither of us allowed it to damage our friendship.

9. Speech at the Conservative Party conference, Blackpool, 11 October 1997.

10. Butler Memorial Lecture, 20 April 1999.

11. Richard Hayton, *Reconstructing Conservatism* (Manchester, 2021) p. 48.

12. Bale p. 91.

13. Spicer p. 454.

14. David Cameron, *For the Record* (William Collins, 2019) p. 57.

15. Clarke p. 416.

16. Iain Duncan Smith was the first person ever to be elected

leader of the Conservative Party who had never previously held a ministerial office of any kind.

17. Norman Fowler, *A Political Suicide Note* (Politico's, 2008) p. 198.
18. Stuart Wheeler, *Winning Against the Odds: My Life in Gambling and Politics* (Quiller, 2019) p. 184.
19. *Ibid.* p. 185.
20. Iain Duncan Smith and his wife were subsequently cleared of any wrongdoing by the Parliamentary commissioner for standards.
21. Clarke p. 424.
22. Ben Patterson, *The Conservative Party and Europe* (John Harper Publishing, 2011) p. 248.
23. Private information from Lord Pearson of Rannoch.
24. Bale p. 201.
25. Andrew Adonis (ed.), *Half In Half Out* (Biteback Publishing, 2018) p. 252.
26. *Ibid.* p. 253.
27. Ed Balls, *Speaking Out: Lessons in Life and Politics* (Hutchinson, 2016), p. 185.

8. Cameron's Dilemmas 2005–2016

1. Chris Mullin, with Ruth Winstone (ed.), *Decline & Fall: Diaries 2005–2010* (Profile Books, 2011) p. 43.
2. David Cameron, *For the Record* (William Collins, 2019) p. 42.
3. Now Lord Hannan of Kingsclere.
4. Michael Spicer, *The Spicer Diaries* (Biteback Publishing, 2012) p. 580.
5. Cameron p. 84.
6. Opening address at the Conservative Party conference, Bournemouth, 1 October 2006.

7. Tim Bale, *The Conservative Party from Thatcher to Cameron* (Polity Press, 2016) p. 278.

8. Kate Fall, *The Gatekeeper* (HQ, 2020) p. 289.

9. Stuart Wheeler, *Winning Against the Odds My Life in Gambling and Politics* (Quiller, 2019) p. 211.

10. Oliver Letwin, *Hearts and Minds: The Battle for the Conservative Party from Thatcher to the Present* (Biteback Publishing, 2017) p. 196.

11. The difference between those arriving in this country and those leaving.

12. Robert Ford and Matthew Goodwin, *Revolt on the Right: Explaining Support for the Radical Right in Britain* (Routledge, 2014) pp. 89–90.

13. Wheeler p. 219.

14. Cameron p. 332.

15. *Guardian* (9 December 2011).

16. Now Lord Cooper of Windrush.

17. Anthony Seldon and Peter Snowdon, *Cameron at 10: The Verdict* (William Collins, 2016) p. 177.

18. *Ibid.* p. 177.

19. Cameron pp. 339–40.

20. The European Court of Human Rights deals with cases relating to the European Convention on Human Rights of which Britain was a founding member when it was established in 1950. Among those who played an influential role in its drafting was Sir David Maxwell Fyfe, who as Lord Kilmuir was Lord Chancellor from 1954 to 1962. See Chapter One.

21. *Guardian* (4 May 2012).

22. Private conversation with Andrew Mitchell.

23. Cameron p. 398.

24. Ken Clarke, *Kind of Blue: A Political Memoir* (Pan Books, 2017) p. 474.

25. Stephen Wall, *The Reluctant European* (Oxford University Press, 2020) p. 281.
26. Bloomberg Speech, 23 January 2013.
27. Now Lord Wharton of Yarm.
28. I was among those who defied the whip.
29. Speech at JCB, Staffordshire, 28 November 2014.
30. Hansard, HC vol 605, cols 783–5 (2 February 2016).
31. *The Sun* (2 February 2016).
32. Fall p. 280.
33. His term of office ended on 9 May 2016, just over a month before the referendum was held.

Conclusions

1. Tim Shipman, *All Out War: The Full Story of Brexit* (William Collins, 2016; revised and updated 2017) is one; Craig Oliver, *Unleashing Demons: The Inside Story of Brexit* (Hodder & Stoughton, 2016) is another.
2. Matthew Elliott, 'How Brexit changed us: Keir Starmer is the true architect of Labour's post-Brexit misfortune', *New Statesman* (25 June–1 July 2021).
3. Kate Fall, *The Gatekeeper* (HQ, 2020) p. 285; Oliver p. 160.
4. Anthony Seldon and Peter Snowdon, *Cameron at 10 The Verdict* (William Collins, 2016) pp. 553–4.
5. David Cameron, *For the Record* (William Collins, 2019) p. 666.
6. Oliver p. 11.
7. Vernon Bogdanor, *Britain & Europe in a Troubled World* (Yale University Press, 2020) pp. 106–7.
8. *Financial Times* (3 June 2016).
9. Cameron p. 665.
10. *Ibid.*
11. *Ibid.* p. 667.
12. BBC, *Andrew Marr Show*, 20 January 2018.

13. It will be recalled that when Gordon Brown succeeded Tony Blair as prime minister in 2007, he was widely criticised for not calling an election to win a mandate of his own. His authority was badly damaged as a result. Theresa May would no doubt also have been criticised under similar circumstances.

Acknowledgements

Kenneth Baker and Peter Hennessy suggested to me that I should write this book. I cannot thank them enough for putting the idea into my head and for their encouragement while I have been writing it. I did so during 2020 and 2021. In the difficult circumstances created by the pandemic, I would never have been able to complete the task without the assistance of the staff of the House of Lords Library and, above all, of Parthe Ward. I owe them a huge debt of gratitude above all for this, but also for all the help I have received from them throughout my time as a member of the House of Lords.

I hugely appreciate the help I have received from those who have read and commented on drafts of my manuscript – Kenneth Baker, Mary Jay, Alistair Lexden, Graham Mather, Richard Ryder, and George Young. I am deeply grateful for the care and attention they devoted to this task as well as for the time they have spent sharing information, memories, and ideas with me. Others who, in different ways, have been very helpful include Sarah Biffen, Vernon Bogdanor, Bill Cash, Patrick Cormack, Norman Fowler, Kate Gavron, Dermot Gleeson, David Howell, Caroline Jackson, Robert Jackson, Michael Jopling, Norman Lamont, Ian Lang, Andrew Mitchell MP, Sara Morrison, David Nicholson, Stephen Parkinson, Chris Patten, Malcolm Pearson, Charles Powell, Caroline Ryder, Anthony Teasdale, and Tom Tugendhat MP. I thank them all while taking sole responsibility for how I have interpreted their views and what I have written. I also thank all those, too numerous to mention by name, with whom, over the years, I have discussed issues relating to Britain and the EU. And I pay a special tribute to the late Roy Jenkins, with whom I had the honour to serve as a commissioner in Brussels. He contributed greatly to my thinking about Europe and Britain's place within it, although he might well not have agreed with all that I have written in this book.

I thank Harry Hall at Haus Publishing for his faith in my project and for everything that he and his team have done to bring it to fruition.

My family has been a constant source of inspiration to me. I am most grateful to my sons, James and Gus, for their encouragement, for their responses to the ideas that I have tried out on them, and for reading and commenting on my manuscript. As with all my books, going back to my first in 1968, my greatest support has been my wife, Julia. She has been behind me, beside me, and spurring me on at every step of the way. I have shared all my ideas with her, and she has read every word I have written before anyone else. We have been together for over fifty years, and there are no words to express the love and the gratitude that I feel for her.

Index